Building *the* Best
YOU

A TWO-YEAR

DISCOVERY

JOURNAL

Caroline Harper

STERLING

New York / London
www.sterlingpublishing.com

STERLING and the distinctive Sterling logo are registered trademarks of Sterling Publishing Co., Inc.

Library of Congress Cataloging-in-Publication Data Available

10 9 8 7 6 5 4 3 2 1

Published by Sterling Publishing Co., Inc.
387 Park Avenue South, New York, NY 10016
© 2008 by Sterling Publishing Co., Inc.

Distributed in Canada by Sterling Publishing
c/o Canadian Manda Group, 165 Dufferin Street
Toronto, Ontario, Canada M6K 3H6
Distributed in the United Kingdom by GMC Distribution Services
Castle Place, 166 High Street, Lewes, East Sussex, England BN7 1XU
Distributed in Australia by Capricorn Link (Australia) Pty. Ltd.
P.O. Box 704, Windsor, NSW 2756, Australia

Printed in China
All rights reserved

ISBN 978-1-4027-6239-0

For information about custom editions, special sales, premium and corporate purchases, please contact Sterling Special Sales Department at 800-805-5489 or specialsales@sterlingpublishing.com.

INTRODUCTION

Building the best YOU there is, and checking in with where you are daily, is the promise. Reclaim your identity and make yourself into the person you have always admired—the person you strive to be. With these basic questions and five minutes of "focus time" a day, you can get there. Not only will you see results from year to year with this two-year journal—you will see a difference from day to day.

Chart your entries and notice patterns. For the first year, fill in the column on the left side of each page. For the second, fill in the column on the right. About every six weeks, you will arrive at a larger set of questions which will prompt you to further reflect on the days past. These questions are spread over two pages and appear twice; fill in the first two pages during the first year, and the second two pages during the second year.

Building the Best YOU doesn't attack and bemoan all that is negative. It helps you highlight the courage, joy, hope, forgiveness, and love that live inside. This journal helps you mine these treasures that are so often out of reach.

Build the things that make a *life worth living* your priority. Notice the negative things you say to yourself. Try an exercise: pretend the negatives were said by someone "whose mission in life was to make [you] miserable," and then fight back. That way, says Martin Seligman, "you don't blindly accept your own insults."

Nurture your strengths, not your negativity.

Nurture human virtues: Satisfaction, Contentment, Fulfillment, Pride, Serenity.

Ask yourself "What's right?" and live your life around those strengths. After inviting this self-discovery process into your life, you will begin to appreciate the little things that you bring to bear and you will build on those strengths. Ultimately those virtues—which are located within but have been brought out on these pages—will spell out the mystical meaning and purpose you have been seeking. You will have built the best YOU there is.

What did I do today?

What did I feel today?

What am I grateful for today?

What challenged me today?

How can I overcome that challenge?

What did I savor today?

What did I do today?

What did I feel today?

What am I grateful for today?

What challenged me today?

How can I overcome that challenge?

What did I savor today?

BUILDING _the_ BEST YOU THERE IS

What did I do today?

_____

_____

_____

What did I feel today?

_____

_____

_____

What am I grateful for today?

_____

_____

_____

What challenged me today?

_____

_____

_____

How can I overcome that challenge?

_____

_____

_____

What did I savor today?

_____

_____

_____

_____

YEAR ONE

What did I do today?

_____

_____

_____

What did I feel today?

_____

_____

_____

What am I grateful for today?

_____

_____

_____

What challenged me today?

_____

_____

_____

How can I overcome that challenge?

_____

_____

_____

What did I savor today?

_____

_____

_____

_____

YEAR TWO

What did I do today?

_____

_____

_____

What did I feel today?

_____

_____

_____

What am I grateful for today?

_____

_____

_____

What challenged me today?

_____

_____

_____

How can I overcome that challenge?

_____

_____

_____

What did I savor today?

_____

_____

_____

_____

What did I do today?

_____

_____

_____

What did I feel today?

_____

_____

_____

What am I grateful for today?

_____

_____

_____

What challenged me today?

_____

_____

_____

How can I overcome that challenge?

_____

_____

_____

What did I savor today?

_____

_____

_____

_____

BUILDING *the* BEST YOU THERE IS

What did I do today?

_____

_____

_____

What did I feel today?

_____

_____

_____

What am I grateful for today?

_____

_____

_____

What challenged me today?

_____

_____

_____

How can I overcome that challenge?

_____

_____

_____

What did I savor today?

_____

_____

_____

What did I do today?

_____

_____

_____

What did I feel today?

_____

_____

_____

What am I grateful for today?

_____

_____

_____

What challenged me today?

_____

_____

_____

How can I overcome that challenge?

_____

_____

_____

What did I savor today?

_____

_____

_____

What did I do today?

What did I feel today?

What am I grateful for today?

What challenged me today?

How can I overcome that challenge?

What did I savor today?

What did I do today?

What did I feel today?

What am I grateful for today?

What challenged me today?

How can I overcome that challenge?

What did I savor today?

BUILDING *the* BEST YOU THERE IS

What did I do today?

_____

_____

_____

_____

What did I feel today?

_____

_____

_____

What am I grateful for today?

_____

_____

_____

What challenged me today?

_____

_____

_____

How can I overcome that challenge?

_____

_____

_____

What did I savor today?

_____

_____

_____

What did I do today?

_____

_____

_____

_____

What did I feel today?

_____

_____

_____

What am I grateful for today?

_____

_____

_____

What challenged me today?

_____

_____

_____

How can I overcome that challenge?

_____

_____

_____

What did I savor today?

_____

_____

_____

What did I do today?

What did I feel today?

What am I grateful for today?

What challenged me today?

How can I overcome that challenge?

What did I savor today?

What did I do today?

What did I feel today?

What am I grateful for today?

What challenged me today?

How can I overcome that challenge?

What did I savor today?

What did I do today?

_____

_____

_____

What did I feel today?

_____

_____

_____

What am I grateful for today?

_____

_____

_____

What challenged me today?

_____

_____

_____

How can I overcome that challenge?

_____

_____

_____

What did I savor today?

_____

_____

_____

YEAR ONE

What did I do today?

_____

_____

_____

What did I feel today?

_____

_____

_____

What am I grateful for today?

_____

_____

_____

What challenged me today?

_____

_____

_____

How can I overcome that challenge?

_____

_____

_____

What did I savor today?

_____

_____

_____

YEAR TWO

What did I do today?

_____

_____

_____

_____

What did I feel today?

_____

_____

_____

_____

What am I grateful for today?

_____

_____

_____

_____

What challenged me today?

_____

_____

_____

_____

How can I overcome that challenge?

_____

_____

_____

_____

What did I savor today?

_____

_____

_____

_____

YEAR ONE

What did I do today?

_____

_____

_____

_____

What did I feel today?

_____

_____

_____

_____

What am I grateful for today?

_____

_____

_____

_____

What challenged me today?

_____

_____

_____

_____

How can I overcome that challenge?

_____

_____

_____

_____

What did I savor today?

_____

_____

_____

_____

YEAR TWO

BUILDING *the* BEST YOU THERE IS

What did I do today?

_____

_____

_____

What did I feel today?

_____

_____

_____

What am I grateful for today?

_____

_____

_____

What challenged me today?

_____

_____

_____

How can I overcome that challenge?

_____

_____

_____

What did I savor today?

_____

_____

_____

What did I do today?

_____

_____

_____

What did I feel today?

_____

_____

_____

What am I grateful for today?

_____

_____

_____

What challenged me today?

_____

_____

_____

How can I overcome that challenge?

_____

_____

_____

What did I savor today?

_____

_____

_____

BUILDING *the* BEST YOU THERE IS

What did I do today?   *What did I do today?*

_____   _____

_____   _____

_____   _____

What did I feel today?   *What did I feel today?*

_____   _____

_____   _____

_____   _____

What am I grateful for today?   *What am I grateful for today?*

_____   _____

_____   _____

_____   _____

What challenged me today?   *What challenged me today?*

_____   _____

_____   _____

_____   _____

How can I overcome that challenge?   *How can I overcome that challenge?*

_____   _____

_____   _____

_____   _____

What did I savor today?   *What did I savor today?*

_____   _____

_____   _____

_____   _____

YEAR ONE   YEAR TWO

BUILDING *the* BEST YOU THERE IS

What did I do today?

_____

_____

_____

What did I feel today?

_____

_____

_____

What am I grateful for today?

_____

_____

_____

What challenged me today?

_____

_____

_____

How can I overcome that challenge?

_____

_____

_____

What did I savor today?

_____

_____

_____

What did I do today?

_____

_____

_____

What did I feel today?

_____

_____

_____

What am I grateful for today?

_____

_____

_____

What challenged me today?

_____

_____

_____

How can I overcome that challenge?

_____

_____

_____

What did I savor today?

_____

_____

_____

What did I do today?

_____

_____

_____

What did I feel today?

_____

_____

_____

What am I grateful for today?

_____

_____

_____

What challenged me today?

_____

_____

_____

How can I overcome that challenge?

_____

_____

_____

What did I savor today?

_____

_____

_____

_____

What did I do today?

_____

_____

_____

What did I feel today?

_____

_____

_____

What am I grateful for today?

_____

_____

_____

What challenged me today?

_____

_____

_____

How can I overcome that challenge?

_____

_____

_____

What did I savor today?

_____

_____

_____

_____

YEAR ONE

YEAR TWO

BUILDING *the* BEST YOU THERE IS

What did I do today?

_____

_____

_____

What did I feel today?

_____

_____

_____

What am I grateful for today?

_____

_____

_____

What challenged me today?

_____

_____

_____

How can I overcome that challenge?

_____

_____

_____

What did I savor today?

_____

_____

_____

What did I do today?

_____

_____

_____

What did I feel today?

_____

_____

_____

What am I grateful for today?

_____

_____

_____

What challenged me today?

_____

_____

_____

How can I overcome that challenge?

_____

_____

_____

What did I savor today?

_____

_____

_____

BUILDING *the* BEST YOU THERE IS

What did I do today?

What did I do today?

_____

_____

_____

_____

_____

_____

What did I feel today?

What did I feel today?

_____

_____

_____

_____

_____

_____

What am I grateful for today?

What am I grateful for today?

_____

_____

_____

_____

_____

_____

What challenged me today?

What challenged me today?

_____

_____

_____

_____

_____

_____

How can I overcome that challenge?

How can I overcome that challenge?

_____

_____

_____

_____

_____

_____

What did I savor today?

What did I savor today?

_____

_____

_____

_____

_____

_____

_____

_____

BUILDING *the* BEST YOU THERE IS

What did I do today?

_____

_____

_____

What did I feel today?

_____

_____

_____

What am I grateful for today?

_____

_____

_____

What challenged me today?

_____

_____

_____

How can I overcome that challenge?

_____

_____

_____

What did I savor today?

_____

_____

_____

YEAR ONE

What did I do today?

_____

_____

_____

What did I feel today?

_____

_____

_____

What am I grateful for today?

_____

_____

_____

What challenged me today?

_____

_____

_____

How can I overcome that challenge?

_____

_____

_____

What did I savor today?

_____

_____

_____

YEAR TWO

What did I do today?

_____

_____

_____

What did I feel today?

_____

_____

_____

What am I grateful for today?

_____

_____

_____

What challenged me today?

_____

_____

_____

How can I overcome that challenge?

_____

_____

_____

What did I savor today?

_____

_____

_____

What did I do today?

_____

_____

_____

What did I feel today?

_____

_____

_____

What am I grateful for today?

_____

_____

_____

What challenged me today?

_____

_____

_____

How can I overcome that challenge?

_____

_____

_____

What did I savor today?

_____

_____

_____

YEAR ONE

YEAR TWO

BUILDING *the* BEST YOU THERE IS

What did I do today?

What did I feel today?

What am I grateful for today?

What challenged me today?

How can I overcome that challenge?

What did I savor today?

What did I do today?

What did I feel today?

What am I grateful for today?

What challenged me today?

How can I overcome that challenge?

What did I savor today?

What did I do today?

What did I do today?

_____

_____

_____

_____

What did I feel today?

What did I feel today?

_____

_____

_____

_____

What am I grateful for today?

What am I grateful for today?

_____

_____

_____

_____

What challenged me today?

What challenged me today?

_____

_____

_____

_____

How can I overcome that challenge?

How can I overcome that challenge?

_____

_____

_____

_____

What did I savor today?

What did I savor today?

_____

_____

_____

_____

_____

_____

What did I do today? _____

_____

_____

_____

What did I feel today? _____

_____

_____

_____

What am I grateful for today? _____

_____

_____

_____

What challenged me today? _____

_____

_____

_____

How can I overcome that challenge? _____

_____

_____

_____

What did I savor today? _____

_____

_____

_____

What did I do today? _____

_____

_____

_____

What did I feel today? _____

_____

_____

_____

What am I grateful for today? _____

_____

_____

_____

What challenged me today? _____

_____

_____

_____

How can I overcome that challenge? _____

_____

_____

_____

What did I savor today? _____

_____

_____

_____

What did I do today?

What did I feel today?

What am I grateful for today?

What challenged me today?

How can I overcome that challenge?

What did I savor today?

What did I do today?

What did I feel today?

What am I grateful for today?

What challenged me today?

How can I overcome that challenge?

What did I savor today?

Date _____

Date _____

What did I do today? _____

_____

_____

_____

What did I feel today? _____

_____

_____

_____

What am I grateful for today? _____

_____

_____

_____

What challenged me today? _____

_____

_____

_____

How can I overcome that challenge? _____

_____

_____

_____

What did I savor today? _____

_____

_____

_____

What did I do today? _____

_____

_____

_____

What did I feel today? _____

_____

_____

_____

What am I grateful for today? _____

_____

_____

_____

What challenged me today? _____

_____

_____

_____

How can I overcome that challenge? _____

_____

_____

_____

What did I savor today? _____

_____

_____

_____

What did I do today?

What did I do today?

What did I feel today?

What did I feel today?

What am I grateful for today?

What am I grateful for today?

What challenged me today?

What challenged me today?

How can I overcome that challenge?

How can I overcome that challenge?

What did I savor today?

What did I savor today?

BUILDING *the* BEST YOU THERE IS

What did I do today?

_____
_____
_____

What did I feel today?

_____
_____
_____

What am I grateful for today?

_____
_____
_____

What challenged me today?

_____
_____
_____

How can I overcome that challenge?

_____
_____
_____

What did I savor today?

_____
_____
_____

YEAR ONE

What did I do today?

_____
_____
_____

What did I feel today?

_____
_____
_____

What am I grateful for today?

_____
_____
_____

What challenged me today?

_____
_____
_____

How can I overcome that challenge?

_____
_____
_____

What did I savor today?

_____
_____
_____

YEAR TWO

BUILDING *the* BEST YOU THERE IS

What did I do today?

What did I do today?

What did I feel today?

What did I feel today?

What am I grateful for today?

What am I grateful for today?

What challenged me today?

What challenged me today?

How can I overcome that challenge?

How can I overcome that challenge?

What did I savor today?

What did I savor today?

YEAR ONE

YEAR TWO

BUILDING *the* BEST YOU THERE IS

What did I do today?

_____

_____

_____

What did I feel today?

_____

_____

_____

What am I grateful for today?

_____

_____

_____

What challenged me today?

_____

_____

_____

How can I overcome that challenge?

_____

_____

_____

What did I savor today?

_____

_____

_____

YEAR ONE

What did I do today?

_____

_____

_____

What did I feel today?

_____

_____

_____

What am I grateful for today?

_____

_____

_____

What challenged me today?

_____

_____

_____

How can I overcome that challenge?

_____

_____

_____

What did I savor today?

_____

_____

_____

YEAR TWO

_____ Date

What did I do today? _____

_____

_____

_____

What did I feel today? _____

_____

_____

_____

What am I grateful for today? _____

_____

_____

_____

What challenged me today? _____

_____

_____

_____

How can I overcome that challenge? _____

_____

_____

_____

What did I savor today? _____

_____

_____

_____

YEAR ONE

_____ Date

What did I do today? _____

_____

_____

_____

What did I feel today? _____

_____

_____

_____

What am I grateful for today? _____

_____

_____

_____

What challenged me today? _____

_____

_____

_____

How can I overcome that challenge? _____

_____

_____

_____

What did I savor today? _____

_____

_____

_____

YEAR TWO

BUILDING *the* BEST YOU THERE IS

What did I do today?

_____

_____

_____

What did I feel today?

_____

_____

_____

What am I grateful for today?

_____

_____

_____

What challenged me today?

_____

_____

_____

How can I overcome that challenge?

_____

_____

_____

What did I savor today?

_____

_____

_____

What did I do today?

_____

_____

_____

What did I feel today?

_____

_____

_____

What am I grateful for today?

_____

_____

_____

What challenged me today?

_____

_____

_____

How can I overcome that challenge?

_____

_____

_____

What did I savor today?

_____

_____

_____

YEAR ONE

YEAR TWO

BUILDING *the* BEST YOU THERE IS

What did I do today?

_____

_____

_____

What did I feel today?

_____

_____

_____

What am I grateful for today?

_____

_____

_____

What challenged me today?

_____

_____

_____

How can I overcome that challenge?

_____

_____

_____

What did I savor today?

_____

_____

_____

What did I do today?

_____

_____

_____

What did I feel today?

_____

_____

_____

What am I grateful for today?

_____

_____

_____

What challenged me today?

_____

_____

_____

How can I overcome that challenge?

_____

_____

_____

What did I savor today?

_____

_____

_____

YEAR ONE

YEAR TWO

What did I do today?

What did I do today?

_____

_____

_____

_____

_____

_____

_____

_____

What did I feel today?

What did I feel today?

_____

_____

_____

_____

_____

_____

_____

_____

What am I grateful for today?

What am I grateful for today?

_____

_____

_____

_____

_____

_____

_____

_____

What challenged me today?

What challenged me today?

_____

_____

_____

_____

_____

_____

_____

_____

How can I overcome that challenge?

How can I overcome that challenge?

_____

_____

_____

_____

_____

_____

_____

_____

What did I savor today?

What did I savor today?

_____

_____

_____

_____

_____

_____

_____

_____

YEAR ONE

YEAR TWO

BUILDING *the* BEST YOU THERE IS

Date

What did I do today?

_____

_____

_____

What did I feel today?

_____

_____

_____

What am I grateful for today?

_____

_____

_____

What challenged me today?

_____

_____

_____

How can I overcome that challenge?

_____

_____

_____

What did I savor today?

_____

_____

_____

Date

What did I do today?

_____

_____

_____

What did I feel today?

_____

_____

_____

What am I grateful for today?

_____

_____

_____

What challenged me today?

_____

_____

_____

How can I overcome that challenge?

_____

_____

_____

What did I savor today?

_____

_____

_____

BUILDING _the_ BEST YOU THERE IS

Date

What did I do today?

What did I feel today?

What am I grateful for today?

What challenged me today?

How can I overcome that challenge?

What did I savor today?

Date

What did I do today?

What did I feel today?

What am I grateful for today?

What challenged me today?

How can I overcome that challenge?

What did I savor today?

BUILDING _the_ BEST YOU THERE IS

What did I do today? _____

_____

_____

_____

What did I feel today? _____

_____

_____

_____

What am I grateful for today? _____

_____

_____

_____

What challenged me today? _____

_____

_____

_____

How can I overcome that challenge? _____

_____

_____

_____

What did I savor today? _____

_____

_____

_____

What did I do today? _____

_____

_____

_____

What did I feel today? _____

_____

_____

_____

What am I grateful for today? _____

_____

_____

_____

What challenged me today? _____

_____

_____

_____

How can I overcome that challenge? _____

_____

_____

_____

What did I savor today? _____

_____

_____

_____

BUILDING *the* BEST YOU THERE IS

What did I do today? _____

_____

_____

_____

What did I feel today? _____

_____

_____

_____

What am I grateful for today? _____

_____

_____

_____

What challenged me today? _____

_____

_____

_____

How can I overcome that challenge? _____

_____

_____

_____

What did I savor today? _____

_____

_____

_____

What did I do today? _____

_____

_____

_____

What did I feel today? _____

_____

_____

_____

What am I grateful for today? _____

_____

_____

_____

What challenged me today? _____

_____

_____

_____

How can I overcome that challenge? _____

_____

_____

_____

What did I savor today? _____

_____

_____

_____

YEAR ONE

YEAR TWO

BUILDING *the* BEST YOU THERE IS

What did I do today?

What did I feel today?

What am I grateful for today?

What challenged me today?

How can I overcome that challenge?

What did I savor today?

What did I do today?

What did I feel today?

What am I grateful for today?

What challenged me today?

How can I overcome that challenge?

What did I savor today?

YEAR ONE

YEAR TWO

BUILDING *the* BEST YOU THERE IS

What did I do today?

_____

_____

_____

_____

What did I feel today?

_____

_____

_____

What am I grateful for today?

_____

_____

_____

What challenged me today?

_____

_____

_____

How can I overcome that challenge?

_____

_____

_____

What did I savor today?

_____

_____

_____

What did I do today?

_____

_____

_____

_____

What did I feel today?

_____

_____

_____

What am I grateful for today?

_____

_____

_____

What challenged me today?

_____

_____

_____

How can I overcome that challenge?

_____

_____

_____

What did I savor today?

_____

_____

_____

What did I do today?

_____

_____

_____

What did I feel today?

_____

_____

_____

What am I grateful for today?

_____

_____

_____

What challenged me today?

_____

_____

_____

How can I overcome that challenge?

_____

_____

_____

What did I savor today?

_____

_____

_____

_____

What did I do today?

_____

_____

_____

What did I feel today?

_____

_____

_____

What am I grateful for today?

_____

_____

_____

What challenged me today?

_____

_____

_____

How can I overcome that challenge?

_____

_____

_____

What did I savor today?

_____

_____

_____

_____

YEAR ONE

YEAR TWO

BUILDING *the* BEST YOU THERE IS

What did I do today?

_____

_____

_____

What did I feel today?

_____

_____

_____

What am I grateful for today?

_____

_____

_____

What challenged me today?

_____

_____

_____

How can I overcome that challenge?

_____

_____

_____

What did I savor today?

_____

_____

_____

YEAR ONE

What did I do today?

_____

_____

_____

What did I feel today?

_____

_____

_____

What am I grateful for today?

_____

_____

_____

What challenged me today?

_____

_____

_____

How can I overcome that challenge?

_____

_____

_____

What did I savor today?

_____

_____

_____

YEAR TWO

What did I do today?

_____

_____

_____

What did I feel today?

_____

_____

_____

What am I grateful for today?

_____

_____

_____

What challenged me today?

_____

_____

_____

How can I overcome that challenge?

_____

_____

_____

What did I savor today?

_____

_____

_____

_____

YEAR ONE

What did I do today?

_____

_____

_____

What did I feel today?

_____

_____

_____

What am I grateful for today?

_____

_____

_____

What challenged me today?

_____

_____

_____

How can I overcome that challenge?

_____

_____

_____

What did I savor today?

_____

_____

_____

_____

YEAR TWO

What did I do today? _____

_____

_____

_____

What did I feel today? _____

_____

_____

_____

What am I grateful for today? _____

_____

_____

_____

What challenged me today? _____

_____

_____

_____

How can I overcome that challenge? _____

_____

_____

_____

What did I savor today? _____

_____

_____

_____

What did I do today? _____

_____

_____

_____

What did I feel today? _____

_____

_____

_____

What am I grateful for today? _____

_____

_____

_____

What challenged me today? _____

_____

_____

_____

How can I overcome that challenge? _____

_____

_____

_____

What did I savor today? _____

_____

_____

_____

YEAR ONE

YEAR TWO

BUILDING _the_ BEST YOU THERE IS

What did I do today?

_____

_____

_____

What did I feel today?

_____

_____

_____

What am I grateful for today?

_____

_____

_____

What challenged me today?

_____

_____

_____

How can I overcome that challenge?

_____

_____

_____

What did I savor today?

_____

_____

_____

_____

What did I do today?

_____

_____

_____

What did I feel today?

_____

_____

_____

What am I grateful for today?

_____

_____

_____

What challenged me today?

_____

_____

_____

How can I overcome that challenge?

_____

_____

_____

What did I savor today?

_____

_____

_____

_____

_____ Date

What did I do today?

_____
_____
_____
_____

What did I feel today?

_____
_____
_____
_____

What am I grateful for today?

_____
_____
_____
_____

What challenged me today?

_____
_____
_____
_____

How can I overcome that challenge?

_____
_____
_____
_____

What did I savor today?

_____
_____
_____
_____

YEAR ONE

_____ Date

What did I do today?

_____
_____
_____
_____

What did I feel today?

_____
_____
_____
_____

What am I grateful for today?

_____
_____
_____
_____

What challenged me today?

_____
_____
_____
_____

How can I overcome that challenge?

_____
_____
_____
_____

What did I savor today?

_____
_____
_____
_____

YEAR TWO

BUILDING *the* BEST YOU THERE IS

Date

Date

What did I do today?

_____

_____

_____

What did I feel today?

_____

_____

_____

What am I grateful for today?

_____

_____

_____

What challenged me today?

_____

_____

_____

How can I overcome that challenge?

_____

_____

_____

What did I savor today?

_____

_____

_____

What did I do today?

_____

_____

_____

What did I feel today?

_____

_____

_____

What am I grateful for today?

_____

_____

_____

What challenged me today?

_____

_____

_____

How can I overcome that challenge?

_____

_____

_____

What did I savor today?

_____

_____

_____

Y E A R O N E

Y E A R T W O

What did I do today?

_____

_____

_____

What did I feel today?

_____

_____

_____

What am I grateful for today?

_____

_____

_____

What challenged me today?

_____

_____

_____

How can I overcome that challenge?

_____

_____

_____

What did I savor today?

_____

_____

_____

YEAR ONE

What did I do today?

_____

_____

_____

What did I feel today?

_____

_____

_____

What am I grateful for today?

_____

_____

_____

What challenged me today?

_____

_____

_____

How can I overcome that challenge?

_____

_____

_____

What did I savor today?

_____

_____

_____

YEAR TWO

What did I do today?

What did I feel today?

What am I grateful for today?

What challenged me today?

How can I overcome that challenge?

What did I savor today?

What did I do today?

What did I feel today?

What am I grateful for today?

What challenged me today?

How can I overcome that challenge?

What did I savor today?

BUILDING *the* BEST YOU THERE IS

What did I do today?

_____

_____

_____

What did I feel today?

_____

_____

_____

What am I grateful for today?

_____

_____

_____

What challenged me today?

_____

_____

_____

How can I overcome that challenge?

_____

_____

_____

What did I savor today?

_____

_____

_____

What did I do today?

_____

_____

_____

What did I feel today?

_____

_____

_____

What am I grateful for today?

_____

_____

_____

What challenged me today?

_____

_____

_____

How can I overcome that challenge?

_____

_____

_____

What did I savor today?

_____

_____

_____

Do I enjoy spending time with others?

_____

_____

_____

_____

_____

Would I like to connect with more people?

_____

_____

_____

_____

_____

Do I feel happy when I'm alone?

_____

_____

_____

_____

_____

Do I feel safe and secure when I'm by myself?

_____

_____

_____

_____

_____

Do I need others to feel whole?

_____

_____

_____

_____

Does my life include other people?

_____

_____

_____

_____

_____

BUILDING *the* BEST YOU THERE IS

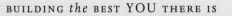

What was my high point in the preceding weeks?

_____

_____

_____

_____

What was my low point?

_____

_____

_____

_____

Did the time flow smoothly?

_____

_____

_____

_____

Did I create goals?

_____

_____

_____

_____

Did I work towards those goals?

_____

_____

_____

_____

Did I achieve those goals?

_____

_____

_____

_____

YEAR

Do I enjoy spending time with others?

_____

_____

_____

_____

Would I like to connect with more people?

_____

_____

_____

_____

Do I feel happy when I'm alone?

_____

_____

_____

_____

Do I feel safe and secure when I'm by myself?

_____

_____

_____

_____

Do I need others to feel whole?

_____

_____

_____

_____

Does my life include other people?

_____

_____

_____

_____

BUILDING *the* BEST YOU THERE IS

What was my high point in the preceding weeks?

_____

_____

_____

What was my low point?

_____

_____

_____

Did the time flow smoothly?

_____

_____

_____

Did I create goals?

_____

_____

_____

Did I work towards those goals?

_____

_____

_____

Did I achieve those goals?

_____

_____

_____

_____

Date _____

What did I do today?

_____

_____

_____

What did I feel today?

_____

_____

_____

What am I grateful for today?

_____

_____

_____

What challenged me today?

_____

_____

_____

How can I overcome that challenge?

_____

_____

_____

What did I savor today?

_____

_____

_____

_____

Date _____

What did I do today?

_____

_____

_____

What did I feel today?

_____

_____

_____

What am I grateful for today?

_____

_____

_____

What challenged me today?

_____

_____

_____

How can I overcome that challenge?

_____

_____

_____

What did I savor today?

_____

_____

_____

_____

Date

What did I do today?

_____

_____

_____

What did I feel today?

_____

_____

_____

What am I grateful for today?

_____

_____

_____

What challenged me today?

_____

_____

_____

How can I overcome that challenge?

_____

_____

_____

What did I savor today?

_____

_____

_____

YEAR ONE

Date

What did I do today?

_____

_____

_____

What did I feel today?

_____

_____

_____

What am I grateful for today?

_____

_____

_____

What challenged me today?

_____

_____

_____

How can I overcome that challenge?

_____

_____

_____

What did I savor today?

_____

_____

_____

YEAR TWO

What did I do today?

_____

_____

_____

_____

What did I feel today?

_____

_____

_____

_____

What am I grateful for today?

_____

_____

_____

_____

What challenged me today?

_____

_____

_____

_____

How can I overcome that challenge?

_____

_____

_____

_____

What did I savor today?

_____

_____

_____

_____

What did I do today?

_____

_____

_____

_____

What did I feel today?

_____

_____

_____

_____

What am I grateful for today?

_____

_____

_____

_____

What challenged me today?

_____

_____

_____

_____

How can I overcome that challenge?

_____

_____

_____

_____

What did I savor today?

_____

_____

_____

_____

YEAR ONE

YEAR TWO

What did I do today?

What did I do today?

What did I feel today?

What did I feel today?

What am I grateful for today?

What am I grateful for today?

What challenged me today?

What challenged me today?

How can I overcome that challenge?

How can I overcome that challenge?

What did I savor today?

What did I savor today?

What did I do today?

What did I do today?

_____

_____

_____

_____

What did I feel today?

What did I feel today?

_____

_____

_____

_____

What am I grateful for today?

What am I grateful for today?

_____

_____

_____

_____

What challenged me today?

What challenged me today?

_____

_____

_____

_____

How can I overcome that challenge?

How can I overcome that challenge?

_____

_____

_____

_____

What did I savor today?

What did I savor today?

_____

_____

_____

_____

_____

_____

What did I do today?

_____

_____

_____

What did I feel today?

_____

_____

_____

What am I grateful for today?

_____

_____

_____

What challenged me today?

_____

_____

_____

How can I overcome that challenge?

_____

_____

_____

What did I savor today?

_____

_____

_____

What did I do today?

_____

_____

_____

What did I feel today?

_____

_____

_____

What am I grateful for today?

_____

_____

_____

What challenged me today?

_____

_____

_____

How can I overcome that challenge?

_____

_____

_____

What did I savor today?

_____

_____

_____

YEAR ONE

YEAR TWO

BUILDING *the* BEST YOU THERE IS

What did I do today? _____

_____

_____

_____

What did I feel today? _____

_____

_____

_____

What am I grateful for today? _____

_____

_____

_____

What challenged me today? _____

_____

_____

_____

How can I overcome that challenge? ____

_____

_____

_____

What did I savor today? _____

_____

_____

_____

What did I do today? _____

_____

_____

_____

What did I feel today? _____

_____

_____

_____

What am I grateful for today? _____

_____

_____

_____

What challenged me today? _____

_____

_____

_____

How can I overcome that challenge? ____

_____

_____

_____

What did I savor today? _____

_____

_____

_____

BUILDING *the* BEST YOU THERE IS

What did I do today?	_What did I do today?_
What did I feel today?	_What did I feel today?_
What am I grateful for today?	_What am I grateful for today?_
What challenged me today?	_What challenged me today?_
How can I overcome that challenge?	_How can I overcome that challenge?_
What did I savor today?	_What did I savor today?_

What did I do today?

What did I do today?

What did I feel today?

What did I feel today?

What am I grateful for today?

What am I grateful for today?

What challenged me today?

What challenged me today?

How can I overcome that challenge?

How can I overcome that challenge?

What did I savor today?

What did I savor today?

BUILDING *the* BEST YOU THERE IS

Date

What did I do today?

What did I feel today?

What am I grateful for today?

What challenged me today?

How can I overcome that challenge?

What did I savor today?

YEAR ONE

Date

What did I do today?

What did I feel today?

What am I grateful for today?

What challenged me today?

How can I overcome that challenge?

What did I savor today?

YEAR TWO

BUILDING _the_ BEST YOU THERE IS

What did I do today?

_____

_____

_____

What did I feel today?

_____

_____

_____

What am I grateful for today?

_____

_____

_____

What challenged me today?

_____

_____

_____

How can I overcome that challenge?

_____

_____

_____

What did I savor today?

_____

_____

_____

_____

What did I do today?

_____

_____

_____

What did I feel today?

_____

_____

_____

What am I grateful for today?

_____

_____

_____

What challenged me today?

_____

_____

_____

How can I overcome that challenge?

_____

_____

_____

What did I savor today?

_____

_____

_____

_____

YEAR ONE

YEAR TWO

BUILDING *the* BEST YOU THERE IS

What did I do today?

_____

_____

_____

What did I feel today?

_____

_____

_____

What am I grateful for today?

_____

_____

_____

What challenged me today?

_____

_____

_____

How can I overcome that challenge?

_____

_____

_____

What did I savor today?

_____

_____

_____

What did I do today?

_____

_____

_____

What did I feel today?

_____

_____

_____

What am I grateful for today?

_____

_____

_____

What challenged me today?

_____

_____

_____

How can I overcome that challenge?

_____

_____

_____

What did I savor today?

_____

_____

_____

YEAR ONE

YEAR TWO

BUILDING *the* BEST YOU THERE IS

What did I do today?

What did I feel today?

What am I grateful for today?

What challenged me today?

How can I overcome that challenge?

What did I savor today?

What did I do today?

What did I feel today?

What am I grateful for today?

What challenged me today?

How can I overcome that challenge?

What did I savor today?

What did I do today?

_____

_____

_____

_____

What did I feel today?

_____

_____

_____

What am I grateful for today?

_____

_____

_____

What challenged me today?

_____

_____

_____

How can I overcome that challenge?

_____

_____

_____

What did I savor today?

_____

_____

_____

What did I do today?

_____

_____

_____

_____

What did I feel today?

_____

_____

_____

What am I grateful for today?

_____

_____

_____

What challenged me today?

_____

_____

_____

How can I overcome that challenge?

_____

_____

_____

What did I savor today?

_____

_____

_____

YEAR ONE

YEAR TWO

BUILDING *the* BEST YOU THERE IS

What did I do today?

_____

_____

_____

What did I feel today?

_____

_____

_____

What am I grateful for today?

_____

_____

_____

What challenged me today?

_____

_____

_____

How can I overcome that challenge?

_____

_____

_____

What did I savor today?

_____

_____

_____

YEAR ONE

What did I do today?

_____

_____

_____

What did I feel today?

_____

_____

_____

What am I grateful for today?

_____

_____

_____

What challenged me today?

_____

_____

_____

How can I overcome that challenge?

_____

_____

_____

What did I savor today?

_____

_____

_____

YEAR TWO

BUILDING *the* BEST YOU THERE IS

What did I do today? _____

_____

_____

_____

_____

What did I feel today? _____

_____

_____

_____

_____

What am I grateful for today? _____

_____

_____

_____

_____

What challenged me today? _____

_____

_____

_____

_____

How can I overcome that challenge? _____

_____

_____

_____

_____

What did I savor today? _____

_____

_____

_____

_____

What did I do today? _____

_____

_____

_____

_____

What did I feel today? _____

_____

_____

_____

_____

What am I grateful for today? _____

_____

_____

_____

_____

What challenged me today? _____

_____

_____

_____

_____

How can I overcome that challenge? _____

_____

_____

_____

_____

What did I savor today? _____

_____

_____

_____

_____

What did I do today?

_____

_____

_____

What did I feel today?

_____

_____

_____

What am I grateful for today?

_____

_____

_____

What challenged me today?

_____

_____

_____

How can I overcome that challenge?

_____

_____

_____

What did I savor today?

_____

_____

_____

_____

What did I do today?

_____

_____

_____

What did I feel today?

_____

_____

_____

What am I grateful for today?

_____

_____

_____

What challenged me today?

_____

_____

_____

How can I overcome that challenge?

_____

_____

_____

What did I savor today?

_____

_____

_____

_____

What did I do today?

What did I do today?

What did I feel today?

What did I feel today?

What am I grateful for today?

What am I grateful for today?

What challenged me today?

What challenged me today?

How can I overcome that challenge?

How can I overcome that challenge?

What did I savor today?

What did I savor today?

BUILDING _the_ BEST YOU THERE IS

What did I do today?

_____

_____

_____

What did I feel today?

_____

_____

_____

What am I grateful for today?

_____

_____

_____

What challenged me today?

_____

_____

_____

How can I overcome that challenge?

_____

_____

_____

What did I savor today?

_____

_____

_____

_____

What did I do today?

_____

_____

_____

What did I feel today?

_____

_____

_____

What am I grateful for today?

_____

_____

_____

What challenged me today?

_____

_____

_____

How can I overcome that challenge?

_____

_____

_____

What did I savor today?

_____

_____

_____

_____

BUILDING *the* BEST YOU THERE IS

What did I do today?

What did I feel today?

What am I grateful for today?

What challenged me today?

How can I overcome that challenge?

What did I savor today?

What did I do today?

What did I feel today?

What am I grateful for today?

What challenged me today?

How can I overcome that challenge?

What did I savor today?

What did I do today?

What did I do today?

What did I feel today?

What did I feel today?

What am I grateful for today?

What am I grateful for today?

What challenged me today?

What challenged me today?

How can I overcome that challenge?

How can I overcome that challenge?

What did I savor today?

What did I savor today?

BUILDING *the* BEST YOU THERE IS

What did I do today?

_____

_____

_____

_____

What did I feel today?

_____

_____

_____

_____

What am I grateful for today?

_____

_____

_____

_____

What challenged me today?

_____

_____

_____

_____

How can I overcome that challenge?

_____

_____

_____

_____

What did I savor today?

_____

_____

_____

_____

What did I do today?

_____

_____

_____

_____

What did I feel today?

_____

_____

_____

_____

What am I grateful for today?

_____

_____

_____

_____

What challenged me today?

_____

_____

_____

_____

How can I overcome that challenge?

_____

_____

_____

_____

What did I savor today?

_____

_____

_____

_____

YEAR ONE

YEAR TWO

BUILDING *the* BEST YOU THERE IS

What did I do today?

What did I do today?

What did I feel today?

What did I feel today?

What am I grateful for today?

What am I grateful for today?

What challenged me today?

What challenged me today?

How can I overcome that challenge?

How can I overcome that challenge?

What did I savor today?

What did I savor today?

What did I do today? _____

_____

_____

_____

What did I feel today? _____

_____

_____

_____

What am I grateful for today? _____

_____

_____

_____

What challenged me today? _____

_____

_____

_____

How can I overcome that challenge? _____

_____

_____

_____

What did I savor today? _____

_____

_____

_____

What did I do today? _____

_____

_____

_____

What did I feel today? _____

_____

_____

_____

What am I grateful for today? _____

_____

_____

_____

What challenged me today? _____

_____

_____

_____

How can I overcome that challenge? _____

_____

_____

_____

What did I savor today? _____

_____

_____

_____

Date

What did I do today?

What did I do today?

What did I feel today?

What did I feel today?

What am I grateful for today?

What am I grateful for today?

What challenged me today?

What challenged me today?

How can I overcome that challenge?

How can I overcome that challenge?

What did I savor today?

What did I savor today?

What did I do today?

_____

_____

_____

_____

What did I feel today?

_____

_____

_____

_____

What am I grateful for today?

_____

_____

_____

_____

What challenged me today?

_____

_____

_____

_____

How can I overcome that challenge?

_____

_____

_____

_____

What did I savor today?

_____

_____

_____

_____

What did I do today?

_____

_____

_____

_____

What did I feel today?

_____

_____

_____

_____

What am I grateful for today?

_____

_____

_____

_____

What challenged me today?

_____

_____

_____

_____

How can I overcome that challenge?

_____

_____

_____

_____

What did I savor today?

_____

_____

_____

_____

What did I do today?

_____

_____

_____

What did I feel today?

_____

_____

_____

What am I grateful for today?

_____

_____

_____

What challenged me today?

_____

_____

_____

How can I overcome that challenge?

_____

_____

_____

What did I savor today?

_____

_____

_____

_____

YEAR ONE

What did I do today?

_____

_____

_____

What did I feel today?

_____

_____

_____

What am I grateful for today?

_____

_____

_____

What challenged me today?

_____

_____

_____

How can I overcome that challenge?

_____

_____

_____

What did I savor today?

_____

_____

_____

_____

YEAR TWO

What did I do today?

_____

_____

_____

_____

What did I feel today?

_____

_____

_____

_____

What am I grateful for today?

_____

_____

_____

_____

What challenged me today?

_____

_____

_____

_____

How can I overcome that challenge?

_____

_____

_____

_____

What did I savor today?

_____

_____

_____

_____

What did I do today?

_____

_____

_____

_____

What did I feel today?

_____

_____

_____

_____

What am I grateful for today?

_____

_____

_____

_____

What challenged me today?

_____

_____

_____

_____

How can I overcome that challenge?

_____

_____

_____

_____

What did I savor today?

_____

_____

_____

_____

What did I do today?

What did I feel today?

What am I grateful for today?

What challenged me today?

How can I overcome that challenge?

What did I savor today?

What did I do today?

What did I feel today?

What am I grateful for today?

What challenged me today?

How can I overcome that challenge?

What did I savor today?

BUILDING *the* BEST YOU THERE IS

_____ Date

What did I do today?

_____
_____
_____
_____

What did I feel today?

_____
_____
_____
_____

What am I grateful for today?

_____
_____
_____
_____

What challenged me today?

_____
_____
_____
_____

How can I overcome that challenge?

_____
_____
_____
_____

What did I savor today?

_____
_____
_____
_____

_____ Date

What did I do today?

_____
_____
_____
_____

What did I feel today?

_____
_____
_____
_____

What am I grateful for today?

_____
_____
_____
_____

What challenged me today?

_____
_____
_____
_____

How can I overcome that challenge?

_____
_____
_____
_____

What did I savor today?

_____
_____
_____
_____

BUILDING *the* BEST YOU THERE IS

What did I do today?

What did I do today?

_____

_____

_____

_____

What did I feel today?

What did I feel today?

_____

_____

_____

_____

What am I grateful for today?

What am I grateful for today?

_____

_____

_____

_____

What challenged me today?

What challenged me today?

_____

_____

_____

_____

How can I overcome that challenge?

How can I overcome that challenge?

_____

_____

_____

_____

What did I savor today?

What did I savor today?

_____

_____

_____

_____

What did I do today?

_____

_____

_____

What did I feel today?

_____

_____

_____

What am I grateful for today?

_____

_____

_____

What challenged me today?

_____

_____

_____

How can I overcome that challenge?

_____

_____

_____

What did I savor today?

_____

_____

_____

What did I do today?

_____

_____

_____

What did I feel today?

_____

_____

_____

What am I grateful for today?

_____

_____

_____

What challenged me today?

_____

_____

_____

How can I overcome that challenge?

_____

_____

_____

What did I savor today?

_____

_____

_____

What did I do today?	*What did I do today?*
What did I feel today?	*What did I feel today?*
What am I grateful for today?	*What am I grateful for today?*
What challenged me today?	*What challenged me today?*
How can I overcome that challenge?	*How can I overcome that challenge?*
What did I savor today?	*What did I savor today?*

Year One	Year Two
What did I do today?	*What did I do today?*
What did I feel today?	*What did I feel today?*
What am I grateful for today?	*What am I grateful for today?*
What challenged me today?	*What challenged me today?*
How can I overcome that challenge?	*How can I overcome that challenge?*
What did I savor today?	*What did I savor today?*

What did I do today?

_____

_____

_____

What did I feel today?

_____

_____

_____

What am I grateful for today?

_____

_____

_____

What challenged me today?

_____

_____

_____

How can I overcome that challenge?

_____

_____

_____

What did I savor today?

_____

_____

_____

What did I do today?

_____

_____

_____

What did I feel today?

_____

_____

_____

What am I grateful for today?

_____

_____

_____

What challenged me today?

_____

_____

_____

How can I overcome that challenge?

_____

_____

_____

What did I savor today?

_____

_____

_____

Y E A R   O N E

Y E A R   T W O

BUILDING *the* BEST YOU THERE IS

What did I do today?

What did I do today?

What did I feel today?

What did I feel today?

What am I grateful for today?

What am I grateful for today?

What challenged me today?

What challenged me today?

How can I overcome that challenge?

How can I overcome that challenge?

What did I savor today?

What did I savor today?

What did I do today?

_____

_____

_____

What did I feel today?

_____

_____

_____

What am I grateful for today?

_____

_____

_____

What challenged me today?

_____

_____

_____

How can I overcome that challenge?

_____

_____

_____

What did I savor today?

_____

_____

_____

_____

BUILDING *the* BEST YOU THERE IS

What did I do today? _____

_____

_____

_____

What did I feel today? _____

_____

_____

_____

What am I grateful for today? _____

_____

_____

_____

What challenged me today? _____

_____

_____

_____

How can I overcome that challenge? _____

_____

_____

_____

What did I savor today? _____

_____

_____

_____

What did I do today? _____

_____

_____

_____

What did I feel today? _____

_____

_____

_____

What am I grateful for today? _____

_____

_____

_____

What challenged me today? _____

_____

_____

_____

How can I overcome that challenge? _____

_____

_____

_____

What did I savor today? _____

_____

_____

_____

What did I do today?

What did I feel today?

What am I grateful for today?

What challenged me today?

How can I overcome that challenge?

What did I savor today?

What did I do today?

What did I feel today?

What am I grateful for today?

What challenged me today?

How can I overcome that challenge?

What did I savor today?

_____ Date

What did I do today? _____

_____
_____
_____

What did I feel today? _____

_____
_____
_____

What am I grateful for today? _____

_____
_____
_____

What challenged me today? _____

_____
_____
_____

How can I overcome that challenge? _____

_____
_____
_____

What did I savor today? _____

_____
_____
_____

_____ Date

What did I do today? _____

_____
_____
_____

What did I feel today? _____

_____
_____
_____

What am I grateful for today? _____

_____
_____
_____

What challenged me today? _____

_____
_____
_____

How can I overcome that challenge? _____

_____
_____
_____

What did I savor today? _____

_____
_____
_____

BUILDING *the* BEST YOU THERE IS

What did I do today?

What did I feel today?

What am I grateful for today?

What challenged me today?

How can I overcome that challenge?

What did I savor today?

What did I do today?

What did I feel today?

What am I grateful for today?

What challenged me today?

How can I overcome that challenge?

What did I savor today?

What did I do today?

What did I do today?

What did I feel today?

What did I feel today?

What am I grateful for today?

What am I grateful for today?

What challenged me today?

What challenged me today?

How can I overcome that challenge?

How can I overcome that challenge?

What did I savor today?

What did I savor today?

BUILDING *the* BEST YOU THERE IS

What did I do today?

What did I feel today?

What am I grateful for today?

What challenged me today?

How can I overcome that challenge?

What did I savor today?

What did I do today?

What did I feel today?

What am I grateful for today?

What challenged me today?

How can I overcome that challenge?

What did I savor today?

What did I do today?

_____

_____

_____

_____

What did I feel today?

_____

_____

_____

_____

What am I grateful for today?

_____

_____

_____

_____

What challenged me today?

_____

_____

_____

_____

How can I overcome that challenge?

_____

_____

_____

_____

What did I savor today?

_____

_____

_____

_____

What did I do today?

_____

_____

_____

_____

What did I feel today?

_____

_____

_____

_____

What am I grateful for today?

_____

_____

_____

_____

What challenged me today?

_____

_____

_____

_____

How can I overcome that challenge?

_____

_____

_____

_____

What did I savor today?

_____

_____

_____

_____

Do I feel loved?

_____

_____

_____

_____

Do I rely on others for love?

_____

_____

_____

_____

Am I in search of deeper love?

_____

_____

_____

_____

Do I know how to achieve deep love?

_____

_____

_____

_____

Am I in touch with my feelings?

_____

_____

_____

_____

What would bring me more love?

_____

_____

_____

_____

_____

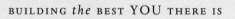

Do I believe in havingness?

_____

_____

_____

_____

Am I creating prosperity?

_____

_____

_____

_____

Could my life be easier?

_____

_____

_____

_____

What can I do to make it easier?

_____

_____

_____

_____

Do I have everything I need?

_____

_____

_____

_____

Do I have everything I want?

_____

_____

_____

_____

Do I feel loved?

_____

_____

_____

_____

_____

Do I rely on others for love?

_____

_____

_____

_____

_____

Am I in search of deeper love?

_____

_____

_____

_____

_____

Do I know how to achieve deep love?

_____

_____

_____

_____

_____

Am I in touch with my feelings?

_____

_____

_____

_____

_____

What would bring me more love?

_____

_____

_____

_____

_____

Do I believe in havingness?

_____

_____

_____

_____

Am I creating prosperity?

_____

_____

_____

_____

Could my life be easier?

_____

_____

_____

_____

What can I do to make it easier?

_____

_____

_____

_____

Do I have everything I need?

_____

_____

_____

_____

Do I have everything I want?

_____

_____

_____

_____

Date

Date

What did I do today?

What did I do today?

_____

_____

_____

_____

_____

_____

What did I feel today?

What did I feel today?

_____

_____

_____

_____

_____

_____

What am I grateful for today?

What am I grateful for today?

_____

_____

_____

_____

_____

_____

What challenged me today?

What challenged me today?

_____

_____

_____

_____

_____

_____

How can I overcome that challenge?

How can I overcome that challenge?

_____

_____

_____

_____

_____

_____

What did I savor today?

What did I savor today?

_____

_____

_____

_____

_____

_____

Year One

Year Two

BUILDING *the* BEST YOU THERE IS

What did I do today?

What did I do today?

What did I feel today?

What did I feel today?

What am I grateful for today?

What am I grateful for today?

What challenged me today?

What challenged me today?

How can I overcome that challenge?

How can I overcome that challenge?

What did I savor today?

What did I savor today?

YEAR ONE

YEAR TWO

BUILDING *the* BEST YOU THERE IS

What did I do today?

_____

_____

_____

What did I feel today?

_____

_____

_____

What am I grateful for today?

_____

_____

_____

What challenged me today?

_____

_____

_____

How can I overcome that challenge?

_____

_____

_____

What did I savor today?

_____

_____

_____

YEAR ONE

What did I do today?

_____

_____

_____

What did I feel today?

_____

_____

_____

What am I grateful for today?

_____

_____

_____

What challenged me today?

_____

_____

_____

How can I overcome that challenge?

_____

_____

_____

What did I savor today?

_____

_____

_____

YEAR TWO

What did I do today?

What did I do today?

_____

_____

_____

What did I feel today?

What did I feel today?

_____

_____

_____

What am I grateful for today?

What am I grateful for today?

_____

_____

_____

What challenged me today?

What challenged me today?

_____

_____

_____

How can I overcome that challenge?

How can I overcome that challenge?

_____

_____

_____

What did I savor today?

What did I savor today?

_____

_____

_____

What did I do today?

_____

_____

_____

What did I feel today?

_____

_____

_____

What am I grateful for today?

_____

_____

_____

What challenged me today?

_____

_____

_____

How can I overcome that challenge?

_____

_____

_____

What did I savor today?

_____

_____

_____

What did I do today?

_____

_____

_____

What did I feel today?

_____

_____

_____

What am I grateful for today?

_____

_____

_____

What challenged me today?

_____

_____

_____

How can I overcome that challenge?

_____

_____

_____

What did I savor today?

_____

_____

_____

YEAR ONE

YEAR TWO

BUILDING *the* BEST YOU THERE IS

What did I do today?

_____

_____

_____

What did I feel today?

_____

_____

_____

What am I grateful for today?

_____

_____

_____

What challenged me today?

_____

_____

_____

How can I overcome that challenge?

_____

_____

_____

What did I savor today?

_____

_____

_____

What did I do today?

_____

_____

_____

What did I feel today?

_____

_____

_____

What am I grateful for today?

_____

_____

_____

What challenged me today?

_____

_____

_____

How can I overcome that challenge?

_____

_____

_____

What did I savor today?

_____

_____

_____

What did I do today?

_____

_____

_____

What did I feel today?

_____

_____

_____

What am I grateful for today?

_____

_____

_____

What challenged me today?

_____

_____

_____

How can I overcome that challenge?

_____

_____

_____

What did I savor today?

_____

_____

_____

_____

What did I do today?

_____

_____

_____

What did I feel today?

_____

_____

_____

What am I grateful for today?

_____

_____

_____

What challenged me today?

_____

_____

_____

How can I overcome that challenge?

_____

_____

_____

What did I savor today?

_____

_____

_____

_____

YEAR ONE

YEAR TWO

Date

Date

What did I do today?

What did I do today?

_____

_____

_____

_____

_____

_____

_____

_____

What did I feel today?

What did I feel today?

_____

_____

_____

_____

_____

_____

What am I grateful for today?

What am I grateful for today?

_____

_____

_____

_____

_____

_____

What challenged me today?

What challenged me today?

_____

_____

_____

_____

_____

_____

How can I overcome that challenge?

How can I overcome that challenge?

_____

_____

_____

_____

_____

_____

What did I savor today?

What did I savor today?

_____

_____

_____

_____

_____

_____

YEAR ONE

YEAR TWO

BUILDING *the* BEST YOU THERE IS

What did I do today?

_____

_____

_____

What did I feel today?

_____

_____

_____

What am I grateful for today?

_____

_____

_____

What challenged me today?

_____

_____

_____

How can I overcome that challenge?

_____

_____

_____

What did I savor today?

_____

_____

_____

_____

What did I do today?

_____

_____

_____

What did I feel today?

_____

_____

_____

What am I grateful for today?

_____

_____

_____

What challenged me today?

_____

_____

_____

How can I overcome that challenge?

_____

_____

_____

What did I savor today?

_____

_____

_____

_____

What did I do today?

What did I feel today?

What am I grateful for today?

What challenged me today?

How can I overcome that challenge?

What did I savor today?

What did I do today?

What did I feel today?

What am I grateful for today?

What challenged me today?

How can I overcome that challenge?

What did I savor today?

BUILDING *the* BEST YOU THERE IS

What did I do today?

What did I do today?

What did I feel today?

What did I feel today?

What am I grateful for today?

What am I grateful for today?

What challenged me today?

What challenged me today?

How can I overcome that challenge?

How can I overcome that challenge?

What did I savor today?

What did I savor today?

BUILDING *the* BEST YOU THERE IS

What did I do today?

_____

_____

_____

What did I feel today?

_____

_____

_____

What am I grateful for today?

_____

_____

_____

What challenged me today?

_____

_____

_____

How can I overcome that challenge?

_____

_____

_____

What did I savor today?

_____

_____

_____

_____

YEAR ONE

What did I do today?

_____

_____

_____

What did I feel today?

_____

_____

_____

What am I grateful for today?

_____

_____

_____

What challenged me today?

_____

_____

_____

How can I overcome that challenge?

_____

_____

_____

What did I savor today?

_____

_____

_____

_____

YEAR TWO

What did I do today?

_____

_____

_____

What did I feel today?

_____

_____

_____

What am I grateful for today?

_____

_____

_____

What challenged me today?

_____

_____

_____

How can I overcome that challenge?

_____

_____

_____

What did I savor today?

_____

_____

_____

What did I do today?

_____

_____

_____

What did I feel today?

_____

_____

_____

What am I grateful for today?

_____

_____

_____

What challenged me today?

_____

_____

_____

How can I overcome that challenge?

_____

_____

_____

What did I savor today?

_____

_____

_____

Date

What did I do today?

_____

_____

_____

_____

What did I feel today?

_____

_____

_____

_____

What am I grateful for today?

_____

_____

_____

_____

What challenged me today?

_____

_____

_____

_____

How can I overcome that challenge?

_____

_____

_____

_____

What did I savor today?

_____

_____

_____

_____

YEAR ONE

Date

What did I do today?

_____

_____

_____

_____

What did I feel today?

_____

_____

_____

_____

What am I grateful for today?

_____

_____

_____

_____

What challenged me today?

_____

_____

_____

_____

How can I overcome that challenge?

_____

_____

_____

_____

What did I savor today?

_____

_____

_____

_____

YEAR TWO

What did I do today?

_____

_____

_____

_____

What did I feel today?

_____

_____

_____

_____

What am I grateful for today?

_____

_____

_____

_____

What challenged me today?

_____

_____

_____

_____

How can I overcome that challenge?

_____

_____

_____

_____

What did I savor today?

_____

_____

_____

_____

What did I do today?

_____

_____

_____

_____

What did I feel today?

_____

_____

_____

_____

What am I grateful for today?

_____

_____

_____

_____

What challenged me today?

_____

_____

_____

_____

How can I overcome that challenge?

_____

_____

_____

_____

What did I savor today?

_____

_____

_____

_____

What did I do today?

_____

_____

_____

What did I feel today?

_____

_____

_____

What am I grateful for today?

_____

_____

_____

What challenged me today?

_____

_____

_____

How can I overcome that challenge?

_____

_____

_____

What did I savor today?

_____

_____

_____

What did I do today?

_____

_____

_____

What did I feel today?

_____

_____

_____

What am I grateful for today?

_____

_____

_____

What challenged me today?

_____

_____

_____

How can I overcome that challenge?

_____

_____

_____

What did I savor today?

_____

_____

_____

What did I do today?	*What did I do today?*

What did I feel today?   *What did I feel today?*

What am I grateful for today?   *What am I grateful for today?*

What challenged me today?   *What challenged me today?*

How can I overcome that challenge?   *How can I overcome that challenge?*

What did I savor today?   *What did I savor today?*

What did I do today?   _What did I do today?_

What did I feel today?   _What did I feel today?_

What am I grateful for today?   _What am I grateful for today?_

What challenged me today?   _What challenged me today?_

How can I overcome that challenge?   _How can I overcome that challenge?_

What did I savor today?   _What did I savor today?_

BUILDING _the_ BEST YOU THERE IS

What did I do today?

What did I do today?

What did I feel today?

What did I feel today?

What am I grateful for today?

What am I grateful for today?

What challenged me today?

What challenged me today?

How can I overcome that challenge?

How can I overcome that challenge?

What did I savor today?

What did I savor today?

BUILDING *the* BEST YOU THERE IS

Date

What did I do today?

_____

_____

_____

What did I feel today?

_____

_____

_____

What am I grateful for today?

_____

_____

_____

What challenged me today?

_____

_____

_____

How can I overcome that challenge?

_____

_____

_____

What did I savor today?

_____

_____

_____

YEAR ONE

Date

What did I do today?

_____

_____

_____

What did I feel today?

_____

_____

_____

What am I grateful for today?

_____

_____

_____

What challenged me today?

_____

_____

_____

How can I overcome that challenge?

_____

_____

_____

What did I savor today?

_____

_____

_____

YEAR TWO

BUILDING *the* BEST YOU THERE IS

What did I do today?

What did I do today?

What did I feel today?

What did I feel today?

What am I grateful for today?

What am I grateful for today?

What challenged me today?

What challenged me today?

How can I overcome that challenge?

How can I overcome that challenge?

What did I savor today?

What did I savor today?

BUILDING *the* BEST YOU THERE IS

What did I do today?

_____

_____

_____

_____

What did I feel today?

_____

_____

_____

_____

What am I grateful for today?

_____

_____

_____

_____

What challenged me today?

_____

_____

_____

_____

How can I overcome that challenge?

_____

_____

_____

_____

What did I savor today?

_____

_____

_____

_____

What did I do today?

_____

_____

_____

_____

What did I feel today?

_____

_____

_____

_____

What am I grateful for today?

_____

_____

_____

_____

What challenged me today?

_____

_____

_____

_____

How can I overcome that challenge?

_____

_____

_____

_____

What did I savor today?

_____

_____

_____

_____

BUILDING *the* BEST YOU THERE IS

What did I do today?

What did I do today?

What did I feel today?

What did I feel today?

What am I grateful for today?

What am I grateful for today?

What challenged me today?

What challenged me today?

How can I overcome that challenge?

How can I overcome that challenge?

What did I savor today?

What did I savor today?

BUILDING *the* BEST YOU THERE IS

What did I do today?

What did I do today?

What did I feel today?

What did I feel today?

What am I grateful for today?

What am I grateful for today?

What challenged me today?

What challenged me today?

How can I overcome that challenge?

How can I overcome that challenge?

What did I savor today?

What did I savor today?

BUILDING *the* BEST YOU THERE IS

What did I do today?

What did I do today?

What did I feel today?

What did I feel today?

What am I grateful for today?

What am I grateful for today?

What challenged me today?

What challenged me today?

How can I overcome that challenge?

How can I overcome that challenge?

What did I savor today?

What did I savor today?

What did I do today?

What did I feel today?

What am I grateful for today?

What challenged me today?

How can I overcome that challenge?

What did I savor today?

What did I do today?

What did I feel today?

What am I grateful for today?

What challenged me today?

How can I overcome that challenge?

What did I savor today?

BUILDING *the* BEST YOU THERE IS

What did I do today?

What did I do today?

What did I feel today?

What did I feel today?

What am I grateful for today?

What am I grateful for today?

What challenged me today?

What challenged me today?

How can I overcome that challenge?

How can I overcome that challenge?

What did I savor today?

What did I savor today?

_____ Date

What did I do today?

_____
_____
_____

What did I feel today?

_____
_____
_____

What am I grateful for today?

_____
_____
_____

What challenged me today?

_____
_____
_____

How can I overcome that challenge?

_____
_____
_____

What did I savor today?

_____
_____
_____

YEAR ONE

_____ Date

What did I do today?

_____
_____
_____

What did I feel today?

_____
_____
_____

What am I grateful for today?

_____
_____
_____

What challenged me today?

_____
_____
_____

How can I overcome that challenge?

_____
_____
_____

What did I savor today?

_____
_____
_____

YEAR TWO

BUILDING *the* BEST YOU THERE IS

Date

What did I do today?

What did I feel today?

What am I grateful for today?

What challenged me today?

How can I overcome that challenge?

What did I savor today?

YEAR ONE

Date

What did I do today?

What did I feel today?

What am I grateful for today?

What challenged me today?

How can I overcome that challenge?

What did I savor today?

YEAR TWO

What did I do today?

What did I do today?

What did I feel today?

What did I feel today?

What am I grateful for today?

What am I grateful for today?

What challenged me today?

What challenged me today?

How can I overcome that challenge?

How can I overcome that challenge?

What did I savor today?

What did I savor today?

BUILDING *the* BEST YOU THERE IS

What did I do today?

What did I do today?

What did I feel today?

What did I feel today?

What am I grateful for today?

What am I grateful for today?

What challenged me today?

What challenged me today?

How can I overcome that challenge?

How can I overcome that challenge?

What did I savor today?

What did I savor today?

What did I do today?   What did I do today?

What did I feel today?   What did I feel today?

What am I grateful for today?   What am I grateful for today?

What challenged me today?   What challenged me today?

How can I overcome that challenge?   How can I overcome that challenge?

What did I savor today?   What did I savor today?

What did I do today?

What did I feel today?

What am I grateful for today?

What challenged me today?

How can I overcome that challenge?

What did I savor today?

What did I do today?

What did I feel today?

What am I grateful for today?

What challenged me today?

How can I overcome that challenge?

What did I savor today?

YEAR ONE   YEAR TWO

BUILDING *the* BEST YOU THERE IS

What did I do today?

What did I do today?

What did I feel today?

What did I feel today?

What am I grateful for today?

What am I grateful for today?

What challenged me today?

What challenged me today?

How can I overcome that challenge?

How can I overcome that challenge?

What did I savor today?

What did I savor today?

BUILDING _the_ BEST YOU THERE IS

What did I do today? _____

What did I do today? _____

_____

_____

_____

_____

_____

_____

What did I feel today? _____

What did I feel today? _____

_____

_____

_____

_____

_____

_____

What am I grateful for today? _____

What am I grateful for today? _____

_____

_____

_____

_____

_____

_____

What challenged me today? _____

What challenged me today? _____

_____

_____

_____

_____

_____

_____

How can I overcome that challenge? _____

How can I overcome that challenge? _____

_____

_____

_____

_____

_____

_____

What did I savor today? _____

What did I savor today? _____

_____

_____

_____

_____

_____

_____

Year One   Year Two

BUILDING *the* BEST YOU THERE IS

What did I do today?   *What did I do today?*

_____   _____

_____   _____

_____   _____

What did I feel today?   *What did I feel today?*

_____   _____

_____   _____

_____   _____

What am I grateful for today?   *What am I grateful for today?*

_____   _____

_____   _____

_____   _____

What challenged me today?   *What challenged me today?*

_____   _____

_____   _____

_____   _____

How can I overcome that challenge? *How can I overcome that challenge?*

_____   _____

_____   _____

_____   _____

What did I savor today?   *What did I savor today?*

_____   _____

_____   _____

_____   _____

What did I do today?

What did I feel today?

What am I grateful for today?

What challenged me today?

How can I overcome that challenge?

What did I savor today?

What did I do today?

What did I feel today?

What am I grateful for today?

What challenged me today?

How can I overcome that challenge?

What did I savor today?

BUILDING *the* BEST YOU THERE IS

What did I do today?

What did I do today?

_____

_____

_____

_____

What did I feel today?

What did I feel today?

_____

_____

_____

_____

What am I grateful for today?

What am I grateful for today?

_____

_____

_____

_____

What challenged me today?

What challenged me today?

_____

_____

_____

_____

How can I overcome that challenge?

How can I overcome that challenge?

_____

_____

_____

_____

What did I savor today?

What did I savor today?

_____

_____

_____

_____

What did I do today?

_____

_____

_____

What did I feel today?

_____

_____

_____

What am I grateful for today?

_____

_____

_____

What challenged me today?

_____

_____

_____

How can I overcome that challenge?

_____

_____

_____

What did I savor today?

_____

_____

_____

What did I do today?

_____

_____

_____

What did I feel today?

_____

_____

_____

What am I grateful for today?

_____

_____

_____

What challenged me today?

_____

_____

_____

How can I overcome that challenge?

_____

_____

_____

What did I savor today?

_____

_____

_____

_____ Date

_____ Date

What did I do today?

_____
_____
_____
_____

What did I feel today?

_____
_____
_____

What am I grateful for today?

_____
_____
_____

What challenged me today?

_____
_____
_____

How can I overcome that challenge?

_____
_____
_____

What did I savor today?

_____
_____
_____

What did I do today?

_____
_____
_____
_____

What did I feel today?

_____
_____
_____

What am I grateful for today?

_____
_____
_____

What challenged me today?

_____
_____
_____

How can I overcome that challenge?

_____
_____
_____

What did I savor today?

_____
_____
_____

YEAR ONE

YEAR TWO

BUILDING *the* BEST YOU THERE IS

What did I do today?

What did I do today?

_____

_____

_____

_____

What did I feel today?

What did I feel today?

_____

_____

_____

_____

What am I grateful for today?

What am I grateful for today?

_____

_____

_____

_____

What challenged me today?

What challenged me today?

_____

_____

_____

_____

How can I overcome that challenge?

How can I overcome that challenge?

_____

_____

_____

_____

What did I savor today?

What did I savor today?

_____

_____

_____

_____

Year One

Year Two

What did I do today?

What did I do today?

What did I feel today?

What did I feel today?

What am I grateful for today?

What am I grateful for today?

What challenged me today?

What challenged me today?

How can I overcome that challenge?

How can I overcome that challenge?

What did I savor today?

What did I savor today?

BUILDING *the* BEST YOU THERE IS

Date

What did I do today?

What did I feel today?

What am I grateful for today?

What challenged me today?

How can I overcome that challenge?

What did I savor today?

What did I do today?

What did I feel today?

What am I grateful for today?

What challenged me today?

How can I overcome that challenge?

What did I savor today?

Date _____

Date _____

What did I do today?
_____
_____
_____
_____

What did I feel today?
_____
_____
_____
_____

What am I grateful for today?
_____
_____
_____
_____

What challenged me today?
_____
_____
_____

How can I overcome that challenge?
_____
_____
_____

What did I savor today?
_____
_____
_____

What did I do today?
_____
_____
_____
_____

What did I feel today?
_____
_____
_____
_____

What am I grateful for today?
_____
_____
_____
_____

What challenged me today?
_____
_____
_____

How can I overcome that challenge?
_____
_____
_____

What did I savor today?
_____
_____
_____

BUILDING *the* BEST YOU THERE IS

_____ *Date*

What did I do today? _____

_____

_____

_____

What did I feel today? _____

_____

_____

_____

What am I grateful for today? _____

_____

_____

_____

What challenged me today? _____

_____

_____

_____

How can I overcome that challenge? _____

_____

_____

_____

What did I savor today? _____

_____

_____

_____

_____

YEAR ONE

_____ *Date*

What did I do today? _____

_____

_____

_____

What did I feel today? _____

_____

_____

_____

What am I grateful for today? _____

_____

_____

_____

What challenged me today? _____

_____

_____

_____

How can I overcome that challenge? _____

_____

_____

_____

What did I savor today? _____

_____

_____

_____

_____

YEAR TWO

What did I do today?

What did I do today?

What did I feel today?

What did I feel today?

What am I grateful for today?

What am I grateful for today?

What challenged me today?

What challenged me today?

How can I overcome that challenge?

How can I overcome that challenge?

What did I savor today?

What did I savor today?

What did I do today?

What did I do today?

_____

_____

_____

_____

What did I feel today?

What did I feel today?

_____

_____

_____

_____

What am I grateful for today?

What am I grateful for today?

_____

_____

_____

_____

_____

_____

What challenged me today?

What challenged me today?

_____

_____

_____

_____

_____

_____

How can I overcome that challenge?

How can I overcome that challenge?

_____

_____

_____

_____

What did I savor today?

What did I savor today?

_____

_____

_____

_____

_____

_____

YEAR ONE

YEAR TWO

What did I do today?   What did I do today?

_____   _____

_____   _____

_____   _____

_____   _____

What did I feel today?   What did I feel today?

_____   _____

_____   _____

_____   _____

What am I grateful for today?   What am I grateful for today?

_____   _____

_____   _____

_____   _____

What challenged me today?   What challenged me today?

_____   _____

_____   _____

_____   _____

How can I overcome that challenge?   How can I overcome that challenge?

_____   _____

_____   _____

_____   _____

What did I savor today?   What did I savor today?

_____   _____

_____   _____

_____   _____

What do I value most in life?

_____

_____

_____

_____

Am I influenced by material things?

_____

_____

_____

_____

Do I treasure family?

_____

_____

_____

_____

What do I admire most about others?

_____

_____

_____

_____

How do I picture myself in twenty years?

_____

_____

_____

_____

How do I get there?

_____

_____

_____

_____

_____

Am I bound to the past?

_____

_____

_____

_____

Do I repeat old patterns?

_____

_____

_____

_____

Do I long for a new direction?

_____

_____

_____

_____

What is that direction?

_____

_____

_____

_____

How do I get there?

_____

_____

_____

_____

What's my first step to take?

_____

_____

_____

_____

BUILDING *the* BEST YOU THERE IS

What do I value most in life?

_____

_____

_____

_____

Am I influenced by material things?

_____

_____

_____

_____

Do I treasure family?

_____

_____

_____

_____

What do I admire most about others?

_____

_____

_____

_____

How do I picture myself in twenty years?

_____

_____

_____

_____

How do I get there?

_____

_____

_____

_____

_____

BUILDING *the* BEST YOU THERE IS

Am I bound to the past?

_____

_____

_____

_____

Do I repeat old patterns?

_____

_____

_____

_____

Do I long for a new direction?

_____

_____

_____

_____

What is that direction?

_____

_____

_____

_____

How do I get there?

_____

_____

_____

_____

What's my first step to take?

_____

_____

_____

_____

What did I do today?

What did I do today?

What did I feel today?

What did I feel today?

What am I grateful for today?

What am I grateful for today?

What challenged me today?

What challenged me today?

How can I overcome that challenge?

How can I overcome that challenge?

What did I savor today?

What did I savor today?

What did I do today?

_____

_____

_____

_____

What did I feel today?

_____

_____

_____

_____

What am I grateful for today?

_____

_____

_____

_____

What challenged me today?

_____

_____

_____

_____

How can I overcome that challenge?

_____

_____

_____

_____

What did I savor today?

_____

_____

_____

_____

What did I do today?

_____

_____

_____

_____

What did I feel today?

_____

_____

_____

_____

What am I grateful for today?

_____

_____

_____

_____

What challenged me today?

_____

_____

_____

_____

How can I overcome that challenge?

_____

_____

_____

_____

What did I savor today?

_____

_____

_____

_____

What did I do today?

_____

_____

_____

_____

What did I feel today?

_____

_____

_____

_____

What am I grateful for today?

_____

_____

_____

_____

What challenged me today?

_____

_____

_____

_____

How can I overcome that challenge?

_____

_____

_____

_____

What did I savor today?

_____

_____

_____

_____

What did I do today?

_____

_____

_____

_____

What did I feel today?

_____

_____

_____

_____

What am I grateful for today?

_____

_____

_____

_____

What challenged me today?

_____

_____

_____

_____

How can I overcome that challenge?

_____

_____

_____

_____

What did I savor today?

_____

_____

_____

_____

Year One

Year Two

BUILDING *the* BEST YOU THERE IS

What did I do today?

What did I do today?

_____

_____

_____

_____

What did I feel today?

What did I feel today?

_____

_____

_____

_____

What am I grateful for today?

What am I grateful for today?

_____

_____

_____

_____

What challenged me today?

What challenged me today?

_____

_____

_____

_____

How can I overcome that challenge?

How can I overcome that challenge?

_____

_____

_____

_____

What did I savor today?

What did I savor today?

_____

_____

_____

_____

What did I do today?

What did I do today?

What did I feel today?

What did I feel today?

What am I grateful for today?

What am I grateful for today?

What challenged me today?

What challenged me today?

How can I overcome that challenge?

How can I overcome that challenge?

What did I savor today?

What did I savor today?

What did I do today?

_____

_____

_____

What did I feel today?

_____

_____

_____

What am I grateful for today?

_____

_____

_____

What challenged me today?

_____

_____

_____

How can I overcome that challenge?

_____

_____

_____

What did I savor today?

_____

_____

_____

What did I do today?

_____

_____

_____

What did I feel today?

_____

_____

_____

What am I grateful for today?

_____

_____

_____

What challenged me today?

_____

_____

_____

How can I overcome that challenge?

_____

_____

_____

What did I savor today?

_____

_____

_____

YEAR ONE

YEAR TWO

BUILDING _the_ BEST YOU THERE IS

What did I do today?

What did I do today?

What did I feel today?

What did I feel today?

What am I grateful for today?

What am I grateful for today?

What challenged me today?

What challenged me today?

How can I overcome that challenge?

How can I overcome that challenge?

What did I savor today?

What did I savor today?

BUILDING *the* BEST YOU THERE IS

What did I do today?

What did I do today?

What did I feel today?

What did I feel today?

What am I grateful for today?

What am I grateful for today?

What challenged me today?

What challenged me today?

How can I overcome that challenge?

How can I overcome that challenge?

What did I savor today?

What did I savor today?

YEAR ONE   YEAR TWO

BUILDING *the* BEST YOU THERE IS

What did I do today?

What did I do today?

_____

_____

_____

_____

_____

_____

What did I feel today?

What did I feel today?

_____

_____

_____

_____

_____

_____

What am I grateful for today?

What am I grateful for today?

_____

_____

_____

_____

_____

_____

What challenged me today?

What challenged me today?

_____

_____

_____

_____

_____

_____

How can I overcome that challenge?

How can I overcome that challenge?

_____

_____

_____

_____

_____

_____

What did I savor today?

What did I savor today?

_____

_____

_____

_____

_____

_____

Date

What did I do today?

_____

_____

_____

What did I feel today?

_____

_____

_____

What am I grateful for today?

_____

_____

_____

What challenged me today?

_____

_____

_____

How can I overcome that challenge?

_____

_____

_____

What did I savor today?

_____

_____

_____

Date

What did I do today?

_____

_____

_____

What did I feel today?

_____

_____

_____

What am I grateful for today?

_____

_____

_____

What challenged me today?

_____

_____

_____

How can I overcome that challenge?

_____

_____

_____

What did I savor today?

_____

_____

_____

BUILDING _the_ BEST YOU THERE IS

What did I do today?

What did I do today?

What did I feel today?

What did I feel today?

What am I grateful for today?

What am I grateful for today?

What challenged me today?

What challenged me today?

How can I overcome that challenge?

How can I overcome that challenge?

What did I savor today?

What did I savor today?

BUILDING *the* BEST YOU THERE IS

_____ Date

_____ Date

What did I do today?

_____

_____

_____

_____

What did I feel today?

_____

_____

_____

What am I grateful for today?

_____

_____

_____

What challenged me today?

_____

_____

_____

How can I overcome that challenge?

_____

_____

_____

What did I savor today?

_____

_____

_____

What did I do today?

_____

_____

_____

_____

What did I feel today?

_____

_____

_____

What am I grateful for today?

_____

_____

_____

What challenged me today?

_____

_____

_____

How can I overcome that challenge?

_____

_____

_____

What did I savor today?

_____

_____

_____

What did I do today? _____

_____

_____

_____

What did I feel today? _____

_____

_____

What am I grateful for today? _____

_____

_____

_____

What challenged me today? _____

_____

_____

_____

How can I overcome that challenge? _____

_____

_____

_____

What did I savor today? _____

_____

_____

_____

What did I do today? _____

_____

_____

_____

What did I feel today? _____

_____

_____

What am I grateful for today? _____

_____

_____

_____

What challenged me today? _____

_____

_____

_____

How can I overcome that challenge? _____

_____

_____

_____

What did I savor today? _____

_____

_____

_____

What did I do today?

_____

_____

_____

What did I feel today?

_____

_____

_____

What am I grateful for today?

_____

_____

_____

What challenged me today?

_____

_____

_____

How can I overcome that challenge?

_____

_____

_____

What did I savor today?

_____

_____

_____

What did I do today?

_____

_____

_____

What did I feel today?

_____

_____

_____

What am I grateful for today?

_____

_____

_____

What challenged me today?

_____

_____

_____

How can I overcome that challenge?

_____

_____

_____

What did I savor today?

_____

_____

_____

YEAR ONE

YEAR TWO

BUILDING *the* BEST YOU THERE IS

What did I do today? _____

_____

_____

_____

_____

What did I feel today? _____

_____

_____

_____

What am I grateful for today? _____

_____

_____

_____

What challenged me today? _____

_____

_____

_____

How can I overcome that challenge? _____

_____

_____

_____

What did I savor today? _____

_____

_____

_____

What did I do today? _____

_____

_____

_____

_____

What did I feel today? _____

_____

_____

_____

What am I grateful for today? _____

_____

_____

_____

What challenged me today? _____

_____

_____

_____

How can I overcome that challenge? _____

_____

_____

_____

What did I savor today? _____

_____

_____

_____

Date

What did I do today?

_____

_____

_____

What did I feel today?

_____

_____

_____

What am I grateful for today?

_____

_____

_____

What challenged me today?

_____

_____

_____

How can I overcome that challenge?

_____

_____

_____

What did I savor today?

_____

_____

_____

Date

What did I do today?

_____

_____

_____

What did I feel today?

_____

_____

_____

What am I grateful for today?

_____

_____

_____

What challenged me today?

_____

_____

_____

How can I overcome that challenge?

_____

_____

_____

What did I savor today?

_____

_____

_____

What did I do today?

What did I do today?

What did I feel today?

What did I feel today?

What am I grateful for today?

What am I grateful for today?

What challenged me today?

What challenged me today?

How can I overcome that challenge?

How can I overcome that challenge?

What did I savor today?

What did I savor today?

What did I do today?

What did I do today?

What did I feel today?

What did I feel today?

What am I grateful for today?

What am I grateful for today?

What challenged me today?

What challenged me today?

How can I overcome that challenge?

How can I overcome that challenge?

What did I savor today?

What did I savor today?

What did I do today?

What did I do today?

What did I feel today?

What did I feel today?

What am I grateful for today?

What am I grateful for today?

What challenged me today?

What challenged me today?

How can I overcome that challenge?

How can I overcome that challenge?

What did I savor today?

What did I savor today?

What did I do today?

What did I do today?

What did I feel today?

What did I feel today?

What am I grateful for today?

What am I grateful for today?

What challenged me today?

What challenged me today?

How can I overcome that challenge?

How can I overcome that challenge?

What did I savor today?

What did I savor today?

BUILDING *the* BEST YOU THERE IS

What did I do today?

What did I do today?

_____

_____

_____

_____

_____

_____

What did I feel today?

What did I feel today?

_____

_____

_____

_____

_____

_____

What am I grateful for today?

What am I grateful for today?

_____

_____

_____

_____

_____

_____

What challenged me today?

What challenged me today?

_____

_____

_____

_____

_____

_____

How can I overcome that challenge?

How can I overcome that challenge?

_____

_____

_____

_____

_____

_____

What did I savor today?

What did I savor today?

_____

_____

_____

_____

_____

_____

What did I do today?

What did I do today?

What did I feel today?

What did I feel today?

What am I grateful for today?

What am I grateful for today?

What challenged me today?

What challenged me today?

How can I overcome that challenge?

How can I overcome that challenge?

What did I savor today?

What did I savor today?

BUILDING *the* BEST YOU THERE IS

What did I do today?

What did I do today?

What did I feel today?

What did I feel today?

What am I grateful for today?

What am I grateful for today?

What challenged me today?

What challenged me today?

How can I overcome that challenge?

How can I overcome that challenge?

What did I savor today?

What did I savor today?

BUILDING *the* BEST YOU THERE IS

What did I do today?

_____

_____

_____

What did I feel today?

_____

_____

_____

What am I grateful for today?

_____

_____

_____

What challenged me today?

_____

_____

_____

How can I overcome that challenge?

_____

_____

_____

What did I savor today?

_____

_____

_____

What did I do today?

_____

_____

_____

What did I feel today?

_____

_____

_____

What am I grateful for today?

_____

_____

_____

What challenged me today?

_____

_____

_____

How can I overcome that challenge?

_____

_____

_____

What did I savor today?

_____

_____

_____

What did I do today?

What did I do today?

What did I feel today?

What did I feel today?

What am I grateful for today?

What am I grateful for today?

What challenged me today?

What challenged me today?

How can I overcome that challenge?

How can I overcome that challenge?

What did I savor today?

What did I savor today?

BUILDING *the* BEST YOU THERE IS

_____ Date   _____ Date

What did I do today? _____   *What did I do today?* _____

_____   _____

_____   _____

_____   _____

What did I feel today? _____   *What did I feel today?* _____

_____   _____

_____   _____

_____   _____

What am I grateful for today? _____   *What am I grateful for today?* _____

_____   _____

_____   _____

_____   _____

What challenged me today? _____   *What challenged me today?* _____

_____   _____

_____   _____

_____   _____

How can I overcome that challenge? ___   *How can I overcome that challenge?* ___

_____   _____

_____   _____

_____   _____

What did I savor today? _____   *What did I savor today?* _____

_____   _____

_____   _____

_____   _____

YEAR ONE   YEAR TWO

BUILDING *the* BEST YOU THERE IS

Date _____

What did I do today? _____

_____

_____

_____

What did I feel today? _____

_____

_____

_____

What am I grateful for today? _____

_____

_____

_____

What challenged me today? _____

_____

_____

_____

How can I overcome that challenge? _____

_____

_____

_____

What did I savor today? _____

_____

_____

_____

Date _____

What did I do today? _____

_____

_____

_____

What did I feel today? _____

_____

_____

_____

What am I grateful for today? _____

_____

_____

_____

What challenged me today? _____

_____

_____

_____

How can I overcome that challenge? _____

_____

_____

_____

What did I savor today? _____

_____

_____

_____

Year One   Year Two

BUILDING _the_ BEST YOU THERE IS

What did I do today?

_____

_____

_____

_____

What did I feel today?

_____

_____

_____

What am I grateful for today?

_____

_____

_____

What challenged me today?

_____

_____

_____

How can I overcome that challenge?

_____

_____

_____

What did I savor today?

_____

_____

_____

_____

What did I do today?

_____

_____

_____

_____

What did I feel today?

_____

_____

_____

What am I grateful for today?

_____

_____

_____

What challenged me today?

_____

_____

_____

How can I overcome that challenge?

_____

_____

_____

What did I savor today?

_____

_____

_____

_____

Date

What did I do today?

_____

_____

_____

What did I feel today?

_____

_____

_____

What am I grateful for today?

_____

_____

_____

What challenged me today?

_____

_____

_____

How can I overcome that challenge?

_____

_____

_____

What did I savor today?

_____

_____

_____

Date

What did I do today?

_____

_____

_____

What did I feel today?

_____

_____

_____

What am I grateful for today?

_____

_____

_____

What challenged me today?

_____

_____

_____

How can I overcome that challenge?

_____

_____

_____

What did I savor today?

_____

_____

_____

BUILDING _the_ BEST YOU THERE IS

What did I do today?

_____

_____

_____

What did I feel today?

_____

_____

_____

What am I grateful for today?

_____

_____

_____

What challenged me today?

_____

_____

_____

How can I overcome that challenge?

_____

_____

_____

What did I savor today?

_____

_____

_____

What did I do today?

_____

_____

_____

What did I feel today?

_____

_____

_____

What am I grateful for today?

_____

_____

_____

What challenged me today?

_____

_____

_____

How can I overcome that challenge?

_____

_____

_____

What did I savor today?

_____

_____

_____

What did I do today?

What did I do today?

What did I feel today?

What did I feel today?

What am I grateful for today?

What am I grateful for today?

What challenged me today?

What challenged me today?

How can I overcome that challenge?

How can I overcome that challenge?

What did I savor today?

What did I savor today?

What did I do today?

What did I feel today?

What am I grateful for today?

What challenged me today?

How can I overcome that challenge?

What did I savor today?

What did I do today?

What did I feel today?

What am I grateful for today?

What challenged me today?

How can I overcome that challenge?

What did I savor today?

YEAR ONE

YEAR TWO

BUILDING *the* BEST YOU THERE IS

What did I do today?

What did I do today?

What did I feel today?

What did I feel today?

What am I grateful for today?

What am I grateful for today?

What challenged me today?

What challenged me today?

How can I overcome that challenge?

How can I overcome that challenge?

What did I savor today?

What did I savor today?

BUILDING *the* BEST YOU THERE IS

What did I do today?

What did I do today?

What did I feel today?

What did I feel today?

What am I grateful for today?

What am I grateful for today?

What challenged me today?

What challenged me today?

How can I overcome that challenge?

How can I overcome that challenge?

What did I savor today?

What did I savor today?

What did I do today?

What did I do today?

What did I feel today?

What did I feel today?

What am I grateful for today?

What am I grateful for today?

What challenged me today?

What challenged me today?

How can I overcome that challenge?

How can I overcome that challenge?

What did I savor today?

What did I savor today?

YEAR ONE

YEAR TWO

BUILDING *the* BEST YOU THERE IS

Date

What did I do today?

What did I feel today?

What am I grateful for today?

What challenged me today?

How can I overcome that challenge?

What did I savor today?

Date

What did I do today?

What did I feel today?

What am I grateful for today?

What challenged me today?

How can I overcome that challenge?

What did I savor today?

BUILDING _the_ BEST YOU THERE IS

_____ Date

What did I do today? _____

_____

_____

_____

What did I feel today? _____

_____

_____

_____

What am I grateful for today? _____

_____

_____

_____

What challenged me today? _____

_____

_____

_____

How can I overcome that challenge? ____

_____

_____

_____

What did I savor today? _____

_____

_____

_____

Year One

_____ Date

What did I do today? _____

_____

_____

_____

What did I feel today? _____

_____

_____

_____

What am I grateful for today? _____

_____

_____

_____

What challenged me today? _____

_____

_____

_____

How can I overcome that challenge? ____

_____

_____

_____

What did I savor today? _____

_____

_____

_____

Year Two

BUILDING *the* BEST YOU THERE IS

What did I do today?

What did I do today?

What did I feel today?

What did I feel today?

What am I grateful for today?

What am I grateful for today?

What challenged me today?

What challenged me today?

How can I overcome that challenge?

How can I overcome that challenge?

What did I savor today?

What did I savor today?

BUILDING *the* BEST YOU THERE IS

What did I do today?

_____

_____

_____

What did I feel today?

_____

_____

_____

What am I grateful for today?

_____

_____

_____

What challenged me today?

_____

_____

_____

How can I overcome that challenge?

_____

_____

_____

What did I savor today?

_____

_____

_____

What did I do today?

_____

_____

_____

What did I feel today?

_____

_____

_____

What am I grateful for today?

_____

_____

_____

What challenged me today?

_____

_____

_____

How can I overcome that challenge?

_____

_____

_____

What did I savor today?

_____

_____

_____

YEAR ONE

YEAR TWO

_____ Date   _____ Date

What did I do today?   *What did I do today?*

_____   _____

_____   _____

_____   _____

What did I feel today?   *What did I feel today?*

_____   _____

_____   _____

_____   _____

What am I grateful for today?   *What am I grateful for today?*

_____   _____

_____   _____

_____   _____

What challenged me today?   *What challenged me today?*

_____   _____

_____   _____

_____   _____

How can I overcome that challenge?   *How can I overcome that challenge?*

_____   _____

_____   _____

_____   _____

What did I savor today?   *What did I savor today?*

_____   _____

_____   _____

_____   _____

What did I do today?

_____

_____

_____

What did I feel today?

_____

_____

_____

What am I grateful for today?

_____

_____

_____

What challenged me today?

_____

_____

_____

How can I overcome that challenge?

_____

_____

_____

What did I savor today?

_____

_____

_____

What did I do today?

_____

_____

_____

What did I feel today?

_____

_____

_____

What am I grateful for today?

_____

_____

_____

What challenged me today?

_____

_____

_____

How can I overcome that challenge?

_____

_____

_____

What did I savor today?

_____

_____

_____

	Date		Date

What did I do today?

What did I feel today?

What am I grateful for today?

What challenged me today?

How can I overcome that challenge?

What did I savor today?

What did I do today?

What did I feel today?

What am I grateful for today?

What challenged me today?

How can I overcome that challenge?

What did I savor today?

BUILDING *the* BEST YOU THERE IS

What did I do today?   *What did I do today?*

_____   _____

_____   _____

_____   _____

What did I feel today?   *What did I feel today?*

_____   _____

_____   _____

_____   _____

What am I grateful for today?   *What am I grateful for today?*

_____   _____

_____   _____

_____   _____

What challenged me today?   *What challenged me today?*

_____   _____

_____   _____

_____   _____

How can I overcome that challenge?   *How can I overcome that challenge?*

_____   _____

_____   _____

_____   _____

What did I savor today?   *What did I savor today?*

_____   _____

_____   _____

_____   _____

YEAR ONE   YEAR TWO

BUILDING *the* BEST YOU THERE IS

What did I do today?

_____

_____

_____

_____

What did I feel today?

_____

_____

_____

What am I grateful for today?

_____

_____

_____

What challenged me today?

_____

_____

_____

How can I overcome that challenge?

_____

_____

_____

What did I savor today?

_____

_____

_____

_____

What did I do today?

_____

_____

_____

_____

What did I feel today?

_____

_____

_____

What am I grateful for today?

_____

_____

_____

What challenged me today?

_____

_____

_____

How can I overcome that challenge?

_____

_____

_____

What did I savor today?

_____

_____

_____

_____

What do I think of myself?

_____

_____

_____

_____

What do other people think of me?

_____

_____

_____

_____

Do I present my true self to others?

_____

_____

_____

_____

Do I show others that I care?

_____

_____

_____

_____

Do I listen to others?

_____

_____

_____

_____

How can I be more tuned in?

_____

_____

_____

_____

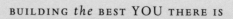

Do I enjoy getting up in the morning?

_____

_____

_____

_____

Do I relish what I do?

_____

_____

_____

_____

Do I look forward to life?

_____

_____

_____

_____

What would resonate more with me?

_____

_____

_____

_____

Do I see the road to fulfillment?

_____

_____

_____

_____

How do I take that path?

_____

_____

_____

_____

BUILDING *the* BEST YOU THERE IS

What do I think of myself?

_____

_____

_____

_____

What do other people think of me?

_____

_____

_____

_____

Do I present my true self to others?

_____

_____

_____

_____

Do I show others that I care?

_____

_____

_____

_____

Do I listen to others?

_____

_____

_____

_____

How can I be more tuned in?

_____

_____

_____

_____

_____

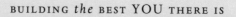

Do I enjoy getting up in the morning?

_____

_____

_____

Do I relish what I do?

_____

_____

_____

Do I look forward to life?

_____

_____

_____

What would resonate more with me?

_____

_____

_____

Do I see the road to fulfillment?

_____

_____

_____

How do I take that path?

_____

_____

_____

_____

Date _____

What did I do today? _____

_____

_____

_____

What did I feel today? _____

_____

_____

_____

What am I grateful for today? _____

_____

_____

_____

What challenged me today? _____

_____

_____

_____

How can I overcome that challenge? _____

_____

_____

_____

What did I savor today? _____

_____

_____

_____

Date _____

What did I do today? _____

_____

_____

_____

What did I feel today? _____

_____

_____

_____

What am I grateful for today? _____

_____

_____

_____

What challenged me today? _____

_____

_____

_____

How can I overcome that challenge? _____

_____

_____

_____

What did I savor today? _____

_____

_____

_____

YEAR ONE

YEAR TWO

BUILDING _the_ BEST YOU THERE IS

What did I do today?

What did I do today?

What did I feel today?

What did I feel today?

What am I grateful for today?

What am I grateful for today?

What challenged me today?

What challenged me today?

How can I overcome that challenge?

How can I overcome that challenge?

What did I savor today?

What did I savor today?

Date

What did I do today?

What did I do today?

What did I feel today?

What did I feel today?

What am I grateful for today?

What am I grateful for today?

What challenged me today?

What challenged me today?

How can I overcome that challenge?

How can I overcome that challenge?

What did I savor today?

What did I savor today?

What did I do today?

What did I do today?

_____

_____

_____

_____

What did I feel today?

What did I feel today?

_____

_____

_____

_____

What am I grateful for today?

What am I grateful for today?

_____

_____

_____

_____

What challenged me today?

What challenged me today?

_____

_____

_____

_____

How can I overcome that challenge?

How can I overcome that challenge?

_____

_____

_____

_____

What did I savor today?

What did I savor today?

_____

_____

_____

_____

BUILDING *the* BEST YOU THERE IS

What did I do today?

What did I feel today?

What am I grateful for today?

What challenged me today?

How can I overcome that challenge?

What did I savor today?

What did I do today?

What did I feel today?

What am I grateful for today?

What challenged me today?

How can I overcome that challenge?

What did I savor today?

What did I do today?

What did I do today?

What did I feel today?

What did I feel today?

What am I grateful for today?

What am I grateful for today?

What challenged me today?

What challenged me today?

How can I overcome that challenge?

How can I overcome that challenge?

What did I savor today?

What did I savor today?

What did I do today?

What did I do today?

_____

_____

_____

_____

_____

_____

_____

_____

What did I feel today?

What did I feel today?

_____

_____

_____

_____

_____

_____

What am I grateful for today?

What am I grateful for today?

_____

_____

_____

_____

_____

_____

What challenged me today?

What challenged me today?

_____

_____

_____

_____

_____

_____

How can I overcome that challenge?

How can I overcome that challenge?

_____

_____

_____

_____

_____

_____

What did I savor today?

What did I savor today?

_____

_____

_____

_____

_____

_____

_____

_____

YEAR ONE

YEAR TWO

BUILDING *the* BEST YOU THERE IS

What did I do today?   *What did I do today?*

_____   _____

_____   _____

_____   _____

What did I feel today?   *What did I feel today?*

_____   _____

_____   _____

_____   _____

What am I grateful for today?   *What am I grateful for today?*

_____   _____

_____   _____

_____   _____

What challenged me today?   *What challenged me today?*

_____   _____

_____   _____

_____   _____

How can I overcome that challenge?   *How can I overcome that challenge?*

_____   _____

_____   _____

_____   _____

What did I savor today?   *What did I savor today?*

_____   _____

_____   _____

_____   _____

What did I do today?

What did I do today?

What did I feel today?

What did I feel today?

What am I grateful for today?

What am I grateful for today?

What challenged me today?

What challenged me today?

How can I overcome that challenge?

How can I overcome that challenge?

What did I savor today?

What did I savor today?

BUILDING *the* BEST YOU THERE IS

Date _____

What did I do today? _____

_____

_____

_____

What did I feel today? _____

_____

_____

_____

What am I grateful for today? _____

_____

_____

_____

What challenged me today? _____

_____

_____

_____

How can I overcome that challenge? _____

_____

_____

_____

What did I savor today? _____

_____

_____

_____

YEAR ONE

Date _____

What did I do today? _____

_____

_____

_____

What did I feel today? _____

_____

_____

_____

What am I grateful for today? _____

_____

_____

_____

What challenged me today? _____

_____

_____

_____

How can I overcome that challenge? _____

_____

_____

_____

What did I savor today? _____

_____

_____

_____

YEAR TWO

BUILDING _the_ BEST YOU THERE IS

What did I do today?

What did I do today?

What did I feel today?

What did I feel today?

What am I grateful for today?

What am I grateful for today?

What challenged me today?

What challenged me today?

How can I overcome that challenge?

How can I overcome that challenge?

What did I savor today?

What did I savor today?

BUILDING *the* BEST YOU THERE IS

What did I do today?

What did I do today?

What did I feel today?

What did I feel today?

What am I grateful for today?

What am I grateful for today?

What challenged me today?

What challenged me today?

How can I overcome that challenge?

How can I overcome that challenge?

What did I savor today?

What did I savor today?

Date

Date

What did I do today?

What did I do today?

What did I feel today?

What did I feel today?

What am I grateful for today?

What am I grateful for today?

What challenged me today?

What challenged me today?

How can I overcome that challenge?

How can I overcome that challenge?

What did I savor today?

What did I savor today?

BUILDING _the_ BEST YOU THERE IS

What did I do today?

What did I do today?

_____

_____

_____

_____

What did I feel today?

What did I feel today?

_____

_____

_____

_____

What am I grateful for today?

What am I grateful for today?

_____

_____

_____

_____

What challenged me today?

What challenged me today?

_____

_____

_____

_____

How can I overcome that challenge?

How can I overcome that challenge?

_____

_____

_____

_____

What did I savor today?

What did I savor today?

_____

_____

_____

_____

Date

What did I do today?

Date

What did I do today?

What did I feel today?

What did I feel today?

What am I grateful for today?

What am I grateful for today?

What challenged me today?

What challenged me today?

How can I overcome that challenge?

How can I overcome that challenge?

What did I savor today?

What did I savor today?

BUILDING _the_ BEST YOU THERE IS

What did I do today?

What did I do today?

What did I feel today?

What did I feel today?

What am I grateful for today?

What am I grateful for today?

What challenged me today?

What challenged me today?

How can I overcome that challenge?

How can I overcome that challenge?

What did I savor today?

What did I savor today?

BUILDING *the* BEST YOU THERE IS

What did I do today?

What did I do today?

What did I feel today?

What did I feel today?

What am I grateful for today?

What am I grateful for today?

What challenged me today?

What challenged me today?

How can I overcome that challenge?

How can I overcome that challenge?

What did I savor today?

What did I savor today?

BUILDING *the* BEST YOU THERE IS

What did I do today?

What did I do today?

What did I feel today?

What did I feel today?

What am I grateful for today?

What am I grateful for today?

What challenged me today?

What challenged me today?

How can I overcome that challenge?

How can I overcome that challenge?

What did I savor today?

What did I savor today?

What did I do today?

What did I do today?

What did I feel today?

What did I feel today?

What am I grateful for today?

What am I grateful for today?

What challenged me today?

What challenged me today?

How can I overcome that challenge?

How can I overcome that challenge?

What did I savor today?

What did I savor today?

YEAR ONE

YEAR TWO

BUILDING *the* BEST YOU THERE IS

What did I do today?

What did I do today?

What did I feel today?

What did I feel today?

What am I grateful for today?

What am I grateful for today?

What challenged me today?

What challenged me today?

How can I overcome that challenge?

How can I overcome that challenge?

What did I savor today?

What did I savor today?

BUILDING *the* BEST YOU THERE IS

Date

What did I do today?

_____

_____

_____

_____

What did I feel today?

_____

_____

_____

What am I grateful for today?

_____

_____

_____

What challenged me today?

_____

_____

_____

How can I overcome that challenge?

_____

_____

_____

What did I savor today?

_____

_____

_____

_____

Date

What did I do today?

_____

_____

_____

_____

What did I feel today?

_____

_____

_____

What am I grateful for today?

_____

_____

_____

What challenged me today?

_____

_____

_____

How can I overcome that challenge?

_____

_____

_____

What did I savor today?

_____

_____

_____

_____

BUILDING *the* BEST YOU THERE IS

What did I do today?

_____

What did I feel today?

_____

What am I grateful for today?

_____

What challenged me today?

_____

How can I overcome that challenge?

_____

What did I savor today?

_____

What did I do today?

_____

What did I feel today?

_____

What am I grateful for today?

_____

What challenged me today?

_____

How can I overcome that challenge?

_____

What did I savor today?

_____

Date

What did I do today?

What did I feel today?

What am I grateful for today?

What challenged me today?

How can I overcome that challenge?

What did I savor today?

Year One

Date

What did I do today?

What did I feel today?

What am I grateful for today?

What challenged me today?

How can I overcome that challenge?

What did I savor today?

Year Two

BUILDING _the_ BEST YOU THERE IS

What did I do today?

What did I do today?

What did I feel today?

What did I feel today?

What am I grateful for today?

What am I grateful for today?

What challenged me today?

What challenged me today?

How can I overcome that challenge?

How can I overcome that challenge?

What did I savor today?

What did I savor today?

YEAR ONE

YEAR TWO

BUILDING *the* BEST YOU THERE IS

What did I do today?

What did I feel today?

What am I grateful for today?

What challenged me today?

How can I overcome that challenge?

What did I savor today?

What did I do today?

What did I feel today?

What am I grateful for today?

What challenged me today?

How can I overcome that challenge?

What did I savor today?

BUILDING *the* BEST YOU THERE IS

What did I do today?

What did I do today?

What did I feel today?

What did I feel today?

What am I grateful for today?

What am I grateful for today?

What challenged me today?

What challenged me today?

How can I overcome that challenge?

How can I overcome that challenge?

What did I savor today?

What did I savor today?

What did I do today?

What did I feel today?

What am I grateful for today?

What challenged me today?

How can I overcome that challenge?

What did I savor today?

What did I do today?

What did I feel today?

What am I grateful for today?

What challenged me today?

How can I overcome that challenge?

What did I savor today?

YEAR ONE

YEAR TWO

BUILDING *the* BEST YOU THERE IS

_____ Date

_____ Date

What did I do today? _____

_____

_____

_____

_____

What did I feel today? _____

_____

_____

_____

What am I grateful for today? _____

_____

_____

_____

What challenged me today? _____

_____

_____

_____

How can I overcome that challenge? _____

_____

_____

_____

What did I savor today? _____

_____

_____

_____

What did I do today? _____

_____

_____

_____

_____

What did I feel today? _____

_____

_____

_____

What am I grateful for today? _____

_____

_____

_____

What challenged me today? _____

_____

_____

_____

How can I overcome that challenge? _____

_____

_____

_____

What did I savor today? _____

_____

_____

_____

BUILDING *the* BEST YOU THERE IS

Date

What did I do today?

What did I feel today?

What am I grateful for today?

What challenged me today?

How can I overcome that challenge?

What did I savor today?

Date

What did I do today?

What did I feel today?

What am I grateful for today?

What challenged me today?

How can I overcome that challenge?

What did I savor today?

What did I do today?　　　　　　　　What did I do today?

What did I feel today?　　　　　　　What did I feel today?

What am I grateful for today?　　　What am I grateful for today?

What challenged me today?　　　　What challenged me today?

How can I overcome that challenge?　　How can I overcome that challenge?

What did I savor today?　　　　　　What did I savor today?

BUILDING *the* BEST YOU THERE IS

What did I do today?

_____

_____

_____

What did I feel today?

_____

_____

_____

What am I grateful for today?

_____

_____

_____

What challenged me today?

_____

_____

_____

How can I overcome that challenge?

_____

_____

_____

What did I savor today?

_____

_____

_____

_____

What did I do today?

_____

_____

_____

What did I feel today?

_____

_____

_____

What am I grateful for today?

_____

_____

_____

What challenged me today?

_____

_____

_____

How can I overcome that challenge?

_____

_____

_____

What did I savor today?

_____

_____

_____

_____

Year One

Year Two

BUILDING *the* BEST YOU THERE IS

Date _____

What did I do today? _____

_____

_____

_____

What did I feel today? _____

_____

_____

What am I grateful for today? _____

_____

_____

What challenged me today? _____

_____

_____

How can I overcome that challenge? _____

_____

_____

What did I savor today? _____

_____

_____

Date _____

What did I do today? _____

_____

_____

_____

What did I feel today? _____

_____

_____

What am I grateful for today? _____

_____

_____

What challenged me today? _____

_____

_____

How can I overcome that challenge? _____

_____

_____

What did I savor today? _____

_____

_____

BUILDING *the* BEST YOU THERE IS

What did I do today?   What did I do today?

What did I feel today?   What did I feel today?

What am I grateful for today?   What am I grateful for today?

What challenged me today?   What challenged me today?

How can I overcome that challenge?   How can I overcome that challenge?

What did I savor today?   What did I savor today?

BUILDING *the* BEST YOU THERE IS

What did I do today?

What did I do today?

What did I feel today?

What did I feel today?

What am I grateful for today?

What am I grateful for today?

What challenged me today?

What challenged me today?

How can I overcome that challenge?

How can I overcome that challenge?

What did I savor today?

What did I savor today?

_____ Date

What did I do today?
_____
_____
_____
_____

What did I feel today?
_____
_____
_____

What am I grateful for today?
_____
_____
_____

What challenged me today?
_____
_____
_____

How can I overcome that challenge?
_____
_____
_____

What did I savor today?
_____
_____
_____

_____ Dat

What did I do today?
_____
_____
_____
_____

What did I feel today?
_____
_____
_____

What am I grateful for today?
_____
_____
_____

What challenged me today?
_____
_____
_____

How can I overcome that challenge?
_____
_____
_____

What did I savor today?
_____
_____
_____

BUILDING *the* BEST YOU THERE IS

What did I do today?

What did I feel today?

What am I grateful for today?

What challenged me today?

How can I overcome that challenge?

What did I savor today?

What did I do today?

What did I feel today?

What am I grateful for today?

What challenged me today?

How can I overcome that challenge?

What did I savor today?

What did I do today?

What did I feel today?

What am I grateful for today?

What challenged me today?

How can I overcome that challenge?

What did I savor today?

What did I do today?

What did I feel today?

What am I grateful for today?

What challenged me today?

How can I overcome that challenge?

What did I savor today?

What did I do today?

_____

_____

_____

What did I feel today?

_____

_____

_____

What am I grateful for today?

_____

_____

_____

What challenged me today?

_____

_____

_____

How can I overcome that challenge?

_____

_____

_____

What did I savor today?

_____

_____

_____

What did I do today?

_____

_____

_____

What did I feel today?

_____

_____

_____

What am I grateful for today?

_____

_____

_____

What challenged me today?

_____

_____

_____

How can I overcome that challenge?

_____

_____

_____

What did I savor today?

_____

_____

_____

What did I do today?   *What did I do today?*

_____   _____

_____   _____

_____   _____

_____   _____

What did I feel today?   *What did I feel today?*

_____   _____

_____   _____

_____   _____

What am I grateful for today?   *What am I grateful for today?*

_____   _____

_____   _____

_____   _____

_____   _____

What challenged me today?   *What challenged me today?*

_____   _____

_____   _____

_____   _____

_____   _____

How can I overcome that challenge?   *How can I overcome that challenge?*

_____   _____

_____   _____

_____   _____

_____   _____

What did I savor today?   *What did I savor today?*

_____   _____

_____   _____

_____   _____

_____   _____

Year One   Year Two

BUILDING *the* BEST YOU THERE IS

What did I do today?

What did I do today?

_____

_____

_____

_____

_____

_____

What did I feel today?

What did I feel today?

_____

_____

_____

_____

_____

_____

What am I grateful for today?

What am I grateful for today?

_____

_____

_____

_____

_____

_____

What challenged me today?

What challenged me today?

_____

_____

_____

_____

_____

_____

How can I overcome that challenge?

How can I overcome that challenge?

_____

_____

_____

_____

_____

_____

What did I savor today?

What did I savor today?

_____

_____

_____

_____

_____

_____

BUILDING *the* BEST YOU THERE IS

What did I do today?

_____

_____

_____

What did I feel today?

_____

_____

_____

What am I grateful for today?

_____

_____

_____

What challenged me today?

_____

_____

_____

How can I overcome that challenge?

_____

_____

_____

What did I savor today?

_____

_____

_____

What did I do today?

_____

_____

_____

What did I feel today?

_____

_____

_____

What am I grateful for today?

_____

_____

_____

What challenged me today?

_____

_____

_____

How can I overcome that challenge?

_____

_____

_____

What did I savor today?

_____

_____

_____

YEAR ONE

YEAR TWO

What did I do today?

What did I do today?

What did I feel today?

What did I feel today?

What am I grateful for today?

What am I grateful for today?

What challenged me today?

What challenged me today?

How can I overcome that challenge?

How can I overcome that challenge?

What did I savor today?

What did I savor today?

BUILDING *the* BEST YOU THERE IS

What did I do today?   *What did I do today?*

_____   _____

_____   _____

_____   _____

What did I feel today?   *What did I feel today?*

_____   _____

_____   _____

_____   _____

What am I grateful for today?   *What am I grateful for today?*

_____   _____

_____   _____

_____   _____

What challenged me today?   *What challenged me today?*

_____   _____

_____   _____

_____   _____

How can I overcome that challenge?   *How can I overcome that challenge?*

_____   _____

_____   _____

_____   _____

What did I savor today?   *What did I savor today?*

_____   _____

_____   _____

_____   _____

BUILDING *the* BEST YOU THERE IS

Date

Date

What did I do today?

What did I do today?

What did I feel today?

What did I feel today?

What am I grateful for today?

What am I grateful for today?

What challenged me today?

What challenged me today?

How can I overcome that challenge?

How can I overcome that challenge?

What did I savor today?

What did I savor today?

What did I do today?

What did I do today?

What did I feel today?

What did I feel today?

What am I grateful for today?

What am I grateful for today?

What challenged me today?

What challenged me today?

How can I overcome that challenge?

How can I overcome that challenge?

What did I savor today?

What did I savor today?

What did I do today?

What did I do today?

What did I feel today?

What did I feel today?

What am I grateful for today?

What am I grateful for today?

What challenged me today?

What challenged me today?

How can I overcome that challenge?

How can I overcome that challenge?

What did I savor today?

What did I savor today?

BUILDING *the* BEST YOU THERE IS

What did I do today?

What did I do today?

What did I feel today?

What did I feel today?

What am I grateful for today?

What am I grateful for today?

What challenged me today?

What challenged me today?

How can I overcome that challenge?

How can I overcome that challenge?

What did I savor today?

What did I savor today?

BUILDING *the* BEST YOU THERE IS

What did I do today?

What did I do today?

What did I feel today?

What did I feel today?

What am I grateful for today?

What am I grateful for today?

What challenged me today?

What challenged me today?

How can I overcome that challenge?

How can I overcome that challenge?

What did I savor today?

What did I savor today?

Do I enjoy spending time with others?

_____

_____

_____

_____

_____

Would I like to connect with more people?

_____

_____

_____

_____

_____

Do I feel happy when I'm alone?

_____

_____

_____

_____

_____

Do I feel safe and secure when I'm by myself?

_____

_____

_____

_____

_____

Do I need others to feel whole?

_____

_____

_____

_____

_____

Does my life include other people?

_____

_____

_____

_____

_____

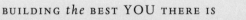

What was my high point in the preceding weeks?

_____

_____

_____

_____

What was my low point?

_____

_____

_____

Did the time flow smoothly?

_____

_____

_____

Did I create goals?

_____

_____

_____

Did I work towards those goals?

_____

_____

_____

Did I achieve those goals?

_____

_____

_____

Do I enjoy spending time with others?

Would I like to connect with more people?

Do I feel happy when I'm alone?

Do I feel safe and secure when I'm by myself?

Do I need others to feel whole?

Does my life include other people?

What was my high point in the preceding weeks?

_____

_____

_____

What was my low point?

_____

_____

_____

Did the time flow smoothly?

_____

_____

_____

Did I create goals?

_____

_____

_____

Did I work towards those goals?

_____

_____

_____

Did I achieve those goals?

_____

_____

_____

_____

What did I do today?

What did I do today?

What did I feel today?

What did I feel today?

What am I grateful for today?

What am I grateful for today?

What challenged me today?

What challenged me today?

How can I overcome that challenge?

How can I overcome that challenge?

What did I savor today?

What did I savor today?

BUILDING *the* BEST YOU THERE IS

What did I do today?

_____

_____

_____

What did I feel today?

_____

_____

_____

What am I grateful for today?

_____

_____

_____

What challenged me today?

_____

_____

_____

How can I overcome that challenge?

_____

_____

_____

What did I savor today?

_____

_____

_____

What did I do today?

_____

_____

_____

What did I feel today?

_____

_____

_____

What am I grateful for today?

_____

_____

_____

What challenged me today?

_____

_____

_____

How can I overcome that challenge?

_____

_____

_____

What did I savor today?

_____

_____

_____

BUILDING *the* BEST YOU THERE IS

What did I do today?

_____

_____

_____

What did I feel today?

_____

_____

_____

What am I grateful for today?

_____

_____

_____

What challenged me today?

_____

_____

_____

How can I overcome that challenge?

_____

_____

_____

What did I savor today?

_____

_____

_____

YEAR ONE

What did I do today?

_____

_____

_____

What did I feel today?

_____

_____

_____

What am I grateful for today?

_____

_____

_____

What challenged me today?

_____

_____

_____

How can I overcome that challenge?

_____

_____

_____

What did I savor today?

_____

_____

_____

YEAR TWO

Date

What did I do today?

What did I feel today?

What am I grateful for today?

What challenged me today?

How can I overcome that challenge?

What did I savor today?

Date

What did I do today?

What did I feel today?

What am I grateful for today?

What challenged me today?

How can I overcome that challenge?

What did I savor today?

What did I do today?

What did I do today?

What did I feel today?

What did I feel today?

What am I grateful for today?

What am I grateful for today?

What challenged me today?

What challenged me today?

How can I overcome that challenge?

How can I overcome that challenge?

What did I savor today?

What did I savor today?

BUILDING *the* BEST YOU THERE IS

Date

What did I do today?

_____

_____

_____

_____

What did I feel today?

_____

_____

_____

What am I grateful for today?

_____

_____

_____

What challenged me today?

_____

_____

_____

How can I overcome that challenge?

_____

_____

_____

What did I savor today?

_____

_____

_____

Date

What did I do today?

_____

_____

_____

_____

What did I feel today?

_____

_____

_____

What am I grateful for today?

_____

_____

_____

What challenged me today?

_____

_____

_____

How can I overcome that challenge?

_____

_____

_____

What did I savor today?

_____

_____

_____

What did I do today?

_____

_____

_____

What did I feel today?

_____

_____

_____

What am I grateful for today?

_____

_____

_____

What challenged me today?

_____

_____

_____

How can I overcome that challenge?

_____

_____

_____

What did I savor today?

_____

_____

_____

_____

What did I do today?

_____

_____

_____

What did I feel today?

_____

_____

_____

What am I grateful for today?

_____

_____

_____

What challenged me today?

_____

_____

_____

How can I overcome that challenge?

_____

_____

_____

What did I savor today?

_____

_____

_____

_____

What did I do today?

What did I do today?

What did I feel today?

What did I feel today?

What am I grateful for today?

What am I grateful for today?

What challenged me today?

What challenged me today?

How can I overcome that challenge?

How can I overcome that challenge?

What did I savor today?

What did I savor today?

BUILDING *the* BEST YOU THERE IS

What did I do today?

What did I do today?

_____

_____

_____

What did I feel today?

What did I feel today?

_____

_____

_____

What am I grateful for today?

What am I grateful for today?

_____

_____

_____

_____

What challenged me today?

What challenged me today?

_____

_____

_____

_____

How can I overcome that challenge?

How can I overcome that challenge?

_____

_____

_____

_____

What did I savor today?

What did I savor today?

_____

_____

_____

_____

Date

What did I do today?

What did I feel today?

What am I grateful for today?

What challenged me today?

How can I overcome that challenge?

What did I savor today?

Date

What did I do today?

What did I feel today?

What am I grateful for today?

What challenged me today?

How can I overcome that challenge?

What did I savor today?

What did I do today?

What did I feel today?

What am I grateful for today?

What challenged me today?

How can I overcome that challenge?

What did I savor today?

What did I do today?

What did I feel today?

What am I grateful for today?

What challenged me today?

How can I overcome that challenge?

What did I savor today?

What did I do today?

What did I do today?

What did I feel today?

What did I feel today?

What am I grateful for today?

What am I grateful for today?

What challenged me today?

What challenged me today?

How can I overcome that challenge?

How can I overcome that challenge?

What did I savor today?

What did I savor today?

BUILDING *the* BEST YOU THERE IS

What did I do today?

What did I do today?

What did I feel today?

What did I feel today?

What am I grateful for today?

What am I grateful for today?

What challenged me today?

What challenged me today?

How can I overcome that challenge?

How can I overcome that challenge?

What did I savor today?

What did I savor today?

BUILDING *the* BEST YOU THERE IS

_____ Date

What did I do today? _____

_____

_____

_____

What did I feel today? _____

_____

_____

What am I grateful for today? _____

_____

_____

What challenged me today? _____

_____

_____

How can I overcome that challenge? _____

_____

_____

What did I savor today? _____

_____

_____

_____ Date

What did I do today? _____

_____

_____

_____

What did I feel today? _____

_____

_____

What am I grateful for today? _____

_____

_____

What challenged me today? _____

_____

_____

How can I overcome that challenge? _____

_____

_____

What did I savor today? _____

_____

_____

YEAR ONE

YEAR TWO

BUILDING the BEST YOU THERE IS

What did I do today?

What did I do today?

What did I feel today?

What did I feel today?

What am I grateful for today?

What am I grateful for today?

What challenged me today?

What challenged me today?

How can I overcome that challenge?

How can I overcome that challenge?

What did I savor today?

What did I savor today?

BUILDING *the* BEST YOU THERE IS

What did I do today?

What did I do today?

What did I feel today?

What did I feel today?

What am I grateful for today?

What am I grateful for today?

What challenged me today?

What challenged me today?

How can I overcome that challenge?

How can I overcome that challenge?

What did I savor today?

What did I savor today?

What did I do today?

What did I do today?

What did I feel today?

What did I feel today?

What am I grateful for today?

What am I grateful for today?

What challenged me today?

What challenged me today?

How can I overcome that challenge?

How can I overcome that challenge?

What did I savor today?

What did I savor today?

BUILDING *the* BEST YOU THERE IS

Date

What did I do today?

Date

What did I do today?

What did I feel today?

What did I feel today?

What am I grateful for today?

What am I grateful for today?

What challenged me today?

What challenged me today?

How can I overcome that challenge?

How can I overcome that challenge?

What did I savor today?

What did I savor today?

Date

What did I do today?

What did I feel today?

What am I grateful for today?

What challenged me today?

How can I overcome that challenge?

What did I savor today?

Date

What did I do today?

What did I feel today?

What am I grateful for today?

What challenged me today?

How can I overcome that challenge?

What did I savor today?

BUILDING _the_ BEST YOU THERE IS

What did I do today?

What did I do today?

What did I feel today?

What did I feel today?

What am I grateful for today?

What am I grateful for today?

What challenged me today?

What challenged me today?

How can I overcome that challenge?

How can I overcome that challenge?

What did I savor today?

What did I savor today?

BUILDING *the* BEST YOU THERE IS

What did I do today?

What did I feel today?

What am I grateful for today?

What challenged me today?

How can I overcome that challenge?

What did I savor today?

What did I do today?

What did I feel today?

What am I grateful for today?

What challenged me today?

How can I overcome that challenge?

What did I savor today?

BUILDING *the* BEST YOU THERE IS

What did I do today?

What did I do today?

What did I feel today?

What did I feel today?

What am I grateful for today?

What am I grateful for today?

What challenged me today?

What challenged me today?

How can I overcome that challenge?

How can I overcome that challenge?

What did I savor today?

What did I savor today?

YEAR ONE

YEAR TWO

BUILDING *the* BEST YOU THERE IS

What did I do today?

What did I do today?

What did I feel today?

What did I feel today?

What am I grateful for today?

What am I grateful for today?

What challenged me today?

What challenged me today?

How can I overcome that challenge?

How can I overcome that challenge?

What did I savor today?

What did I savor today?

BUILDING *the* BEST YOU THERE IS

What did I do today?

What did I do today?

What did I feel today?

What did I feel today?

What am I grateful for today?

What am I grateful for today?

What challenged me today?

What challenged me today?

How can I overcome that challenge?

How can I overcome that challenge?

What did I savor today?

What did I savor today?

YEAR ONE

YEAR TWO

BUILDING *the* BEST YOU THERE IS

What did I do today?

_____

_____

_____

What did I feel today?

_____

_____

_____

What am I grateful for today?

_____

_____

_____

What challenged me today?

_____

_____

_____

How can I overcome that challenge?

_____

_____

_____

What did I savor today?

_____

_____

_____

_____

What did I do today?

_____

_____

_____

What did I feel today?

_____

_____

_____

What am I grateful for today?

_____

_____

_____

What challenged me today?

_____

_____

_____

How can I overcome that challenge?

_____

_____

_____

What did I savor today?

_____

_____

_____

_____

What did I do today?

_____

_____

_____

What did I feel today?

_____

_____

_____

What am I grateful for today?

_____

_____

_____

What challenged me today?

_____

_____

_____

How can I overcome that challenge?

_____

_____

_____

What did I savor today?

_____

_____

_____

What did I do today?

_____

_____

_____

What did I feel today?

_____

_____

_____

What am I grateful for today?

_____

_____

_____

What challenged me today?

_____

_____

_____

How can I overcome that challenge?

_____

_____

_____

What did I savor today?

_____

_____

_____

Year One

Year Two

BUILDING *the* BEST YOU THERE IS

Date _____

Date _____

What did I do today? _____

_____

_____

_____

What did I feel today? _____

_____

_____

_____

What am I grateful for today? _____

_____

_____

_____

What challenged me today? _____

_____

_____

_____

How can I overcome that challenge? _____

_____

_____

_____

What did I savor today? _____

_____

_____

_____

YEAR ONE

What did I do today? _____

_____

_____

_____

What did I feel today? _____

_____

_____

_____

What am I grateful for today? _____

_____

_____

_____

What challenged me today? _____

_____

_____

_____

How can I overcome that challenge? _____

_____

_____

_____

What did I savor today? _____

_____

_____

_____

YEAR TWO

BUILDING *the* BEST YOU THERE IS

What did I do today?

What did I do today?

_____

_____

_____

_____

_____

_____

What did I feel today?

What did I feel today?

_____

_____

_____

_____

_____

_____

What am I grateful for today?

What am I grateful for today?

_____

_____

_____

_____

_____

_____

What challenged me today?

What challenged me today?

_____

_____

_____

_____

_____

_____

How can I overcome that challenge?

How can I overcome that challenge?

_____

_____

_____

_____

_____

_____

What did I savor today?

What did I savor today?

_____

_____

_____

_____

_____

_____

What did I do today? | What did I do today?

_____

_____

_____

What did I feel today? | What did I feel today?

_____

_____

_____

What am I grateful for today? | What am I grateful for today?

_____

_____

_____

What challenged me today? | What challenged me today?

_____

_____

_____

How can I overcome that challenge? | How can I overcome that challenge?

_____

_____

_____

What did I savor today? | What did I savor today?

_____

_____

_____

What did I do today?

What did I do today?

What did I feel today?

What did I feel today?

What am I grateful for today?

What am I grateful for today?

What challenged me today?

What challenged me today?

How can I overcome that challenge?

How can I overcome that challenge?

What did I savor today?

What did I savor today?

BUILDING *the* BEST YOU THERE IS

What did I do today?

What did I feel today?

What am I grateful for today?

What challenged me today?

How can I overcome that challenge?

What did I savor today?

What did I do today?

What did I feel today?

What am I grateful for today?

What challenged me today?

How can I overcome that challenge?

What did I savor today?

Date

Date

What did I do today?

What did I do today?

What did I feel today?

What did I feel today?

What am I grateful for today?

What am I grateful for today?

What challenged me today?

What challenged me today?

How can I overcome that challenge?

How can I overcome that challenge?

What did I savor today?

What did I savor today?

What did I do today?

What did I do today?

What did I feel today?

What did I feel today?

What am I grateful for today?

What am I grateful for today?

What challenged me today?

What challenged me today?

How can I overcome that challenge?

How can I overcome that challenge?

What did I savor today?

What did I savor today?

BUILDING *the* BEST YOU THERE IS

What did I do today?

What did I do today?

What did I feel today?

What did I feel today?

What am I grateful for today?

What am I grateful for today?

What challenged me today?

What challenged me today?

How can I overcome that challenge?

How can I overcome that challenge?

What did I savor today?

What did I savor today?

BUILDING _the_ BEST YOU THERE IS

What did I do today? _____

What did I do today? _____

_____

_____

_____

_____

_____

_____

What did I feel today? _____

What did I feel today? _____

_____

_____

_____

_____

_____

_____

What am I grateful for today? _____

What am I grateful for today? _____

_____

_____

_____

_____

_____

_____

What challenged me today? _____

What challenged me today? _____

_____

_____

_____

_____

_____

_____

How can I overcome that challenge? _____

How can I overcome that challenge? _____

_____

_____

_____

_____

_____

_____

What did I savor today? _____

What did I savor today? _____

_____

_____

_____

_____

_____

_____

_____

_____

Date
Date

What did I do today?

What did I do today?

What did I feel today?

What did I feel today?

What am I grateful for today?

What am I grateful for today?

What challenged me today?

What challenged me today?

How can I overcome that challenge?

How can I overcome that challenge?

What did I savor today?

What did I savor today?

BUILDING *the* BEST YOU THERE IS

What did I do today?   *What did I do today?*

_____   _____

_____   _____

_____   _____

What did I feel today?   *What did I feel today?*

_____   _____

_____   _____

_____   _____

What am I grateful for today?   *What am I grateful for today?*

_____   _____

_____   _____

_____   _____

What challenged me today?   *What challenged me today?*

_____   _____

_____   _____

_____   _____

How can I overcome that challenge?   *How can I overcome that challenge?*

_____   _____

_____   _____

_____   _____

What did I savor today?   *What did I savor today?*

_____   _____

_____   _____

_____   _____

BUILDING *the* BEST YOU THERE IS

What did I do today?

What did I do today?

What did I feel today?

What did I feel today?

What am I grateful for today?

What am I grateful for today?

What challenged me today?

What challenged me today?

How can I overcome that challenge?

How can I overcome that challenge?

What did I savor today?

What did I savor today?

What did I do today?

What did I feel today?

What am I grateful for today?

What challenged me today?

How can I overcome that challenge?

What did I savor today?

What did I do today?

What did I feel today?

What am I grateful for today?

What challenged me today?

How can I overcome that challenge?

What did I savor today?

BUILDING *the* BEST YOU THERE IS

What did I do today?

What did I do today?

What did I feel today?

What did I feel today?

What am I grateful for today?

What am I grateful for today?

What challenged me today?

What challenged me today?

How can I overcome that challenge?

How can I overcome that challenge?

What did I savor today?

What did I savor today?

What did I do today?

What did I feel today?

What am I grateful for today?

What challenged me today?

How can I overcome that challenge?

What did I savor today?

What did I do today?

What did I feel today?

What am I grateful for today?

What challenged me today?

How can I overcome that challenge?

What did I savor today?

What did I do today?

What did I do today?

What did I feel today?

What did I feel today?

What am I grateful for today?

What am I grateful for today?

What challenged me today?

What challenged me today?

How can I overcome that challenge?

How can I overcome that challenge?

What did I savor today?

What did I savor today?

What did I do today?   *What did I do today?*

What did I feel today?   *What did I feel today?*

What am I grateful for today?   *What am I grateful for today?*

What challenged me today?   *What challenged me today?*

How can I overcome that challenge?   *How can I overcome that challenge?*

What did I savor today?   *What did I savor today?*

_____ Date

What did I do today? _____

_____

_____

_____

What did I feel today? _____

_____

_____

_____

What am I grateful for today? _____

_____

_____

_____

What challenged me today? _____

_____

_____

_____

How can I overcome that challenge? _____

_____

_____

_____

What did I savor today? _____

_____

_____

_____

_____ Date

What did I do today? _____

_____

_____

_____

What did I feel today? _____

_____

_____

_____

What am I grateful for today? _____

_____

_____

_____

What challenged me today? _____

_____

_____

_____

How can I overcome that challenge? _____

_____

_____

_____

What did I savor today? _____

_____

_____

_____

BUILDING *the* BEST YOU THERE IS

Do I feel loved?

_____

_____

_____

_____

Do I rely on others for love?

_____

_____

_____

_____

Am I in search of deeper love?

_____

_____

_____

_____

Do I know how to achieve deep love?

_____

_____

_____

_____

Am I in touch with my feelings?

_____

_____

_____

_____

What would bring me more love?

_____

_____

_____

_____

Do I believe in havingness?

_____

_____

_____

_____

Am I creating prosperity?

_____

_____

_____

_____

Could my life be easier?

_____

_____

_____

_____

What can I do to make it easier?

_____

_____

_____

_____

Do I have everything I need?

_____

_____

_____

_____

Do I have everything I want?

_____

_____

_____

_____

Do I feel loved?

Do I rely on others for love?

Am I in search of deeper love?

Do I know how to achieve deep love?

Am I in touch with my feelings?

What would bring me more love?

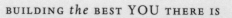

Do I believe in havingness?

_____

_____

_____

_____

Am I creating prosperity?

_____

_____

_____

Could my life be easier?

_____

_____

_____

What can I do to make it easier?

_____

_____

_____

_____

Do I have everything I need?

_____

_____

_____

Do I have everything I want?

_____

_____

_____

_____

What did I do today?   *What did I do today?*

What did I feel today?   *What did I feel today?*

What am I grateful for today?   *What am I grateful for today?*

What challenged me today?   *What challenged me today?*

How can I overcome that challenge?   *How can I overcome that challenge?*

What did I savor today?   *What did I savor today?*

_____ Date

What did I do today?

_____

_____

_____

What did I feel today?

_____

_____

_____

What am I grateful for today?

_____

_____

_____

What challenged me today?

_____

_____

_____

How can I overcome that challenge?

_____

_____

_____

What did I savor today?

_____

_____

_____

YEAR ONE

_____ Date

What did I do today?

_____

_____

_____

What did I feel today?

_____

_____

_____

What am I grateful for today?

_____

_____

_____

What challenged me today?

_____

_____

_____

How can I overcome that challenge?

_____

_____

_____

What did I savor today?

_____

_____

_____

YEAR TWO

What did I do today?

What did I do today?

What did I feel today?

What did I feel today?

What am I grateful for today?

What am I grateful for today?

What challenged me today?

What challenged me today?

How can I overcome that challenge?

How can I overcome that challenge?

What did I savor today?

What did I savor today?

BUILDING *the* BEST YOU THERE IS

What did I do today?

What did I feel today?

What am I grateful for today?

What challenged me today?

How can I overcome that challenge?

What did I savor today?

What did I do today?

What did I feel today?

What am I grateful for today?

What challenged me today?

How can I overcome that challenge?

What did I savor today?

YEAR ONE

YEAR TWO

BUILDING *the* BEST YOU THERE IS

Date _____

What did I do today?
_____
_____
_____
_____
_____

What did I feel today?
_____
_____
_____
_____

What am I grateful for today?
_____
_____
_____
_____

What challenged me today?
_____
_____
_____
_____

How can I overcome that challenge?
_____
_____
_____
_____

What did I savor today?
_____
_____
_____
_____

YEAR ONE

Date _____

What did I do today?
_____
_____
_____
_____
_____

What did I feel today?
_____
_____
_____
_____

What am I grateful for today?
_____
_____
_____
_____

What challenged me today?
_____
_____
_____
_____

How can I overcome that challenge?
_____
_____
_____
_____

What did I savor today?
_____
_____
_____
_____

YEAR TWO

What did I do today?

What did I do today?

What did I feel today?

What did I feel today?

What am I grateful for today?

What am I grateful for today?

What challenged me today?

What challenged me today?

How can I overcome that challenge?

How can I overcome that challenge?

What did I savor today?

What did I savor today?

What did I do today?

What did I do today?

What did I feel today?

What did I feel today?

What am I grateful for today?

What am I grateful for today?

What challenged me today?

What challenged me today?

How can I overcome that challenge?

How can I overcome that challenge?

What did I savor today?

What did I savor today?

BUILDING *the* BEST YOU THERE IS

What did I do today?

What did I do today?

What did I feel today?

What did I feel today?

What am I grateful for today?

What am I grateful for today?

What challenged me today?

What challenged me today?

How can I overcome that challenge?

How can I overcome that challenge?

What did I savor today?

What did I savor today?

BUILDING *the* BEST YOU THERE IS

What did I do today? _____

What did I do today? _____

What did I feel today? _____

What did I feel today? _____

What am I grateful for today? _____

What am I grateful for today? _____

What challenged me today? _____

What challenged me today? _____

How can I overcome that challenge? _____

How can I overcome that challenge? _____

What did I savor today? _____

What did I savor today? _____

YEAR ONE

YEAR TWO

BUILDING _the_ BEST YOU THERE IS

What did I do today?

What did I do today?

What did I feel today?

What did I feel today?

What am I grateful for today?

What am I grateful for today?

What challenged me today?

What challenged me today?

How can I overcome that challenge?

How can I overcome that challenge?

What did I savor today?

What did I savor today?

YEAR ONE

YEAR TWO

BUILDING *the* BEST YOU THERE IS

What did I do today?

What did I do today?

What did I feel today?

What did I feel today?

What am I grateful for today?

What am I grateful for today?

What challenged me today?

What challenged me today?

How can I overcome that challenge?

How can I overcome that challenge?

What did I savor today?

What did I savor today?

BUILDING *the* BEST YOU THERE IS

What did I do today?

What did I do today?

What did I feel today?

What did I feel today?

What am I grateful for today?

What am I grateful for today?

What challenged me today?

What challenged me today?

How can I overcome that challenge?

How can I overcome that challenge?

What did I savor today?

What did I savor today?

BUILDING *the* BEST YOU THERE IS

What did I do today?

What did I do today?

What did I feel today?

What did I feel today?

What am I grateful for today?

What am I grateful for today?

What challenged me today?

What challenged me today?

How can I overcome that challenge?

How can I overcome that challenge?

What did I savor today?

What did I savor today?

BUILDING *the* BEST YOU THERE IS

What did I do today?

_____

_____

_____

_____

What did I feel today?

_____

_____

_____

What am I grateful for today?

_____

_____

_____

What challenged me today?

_____

_____

_____

How can I overcome that challenge?

_____

_____

_____

What did I savor today?

_____

_____

_____

_____

What did I do today?

_____

_____

_____

_____

What did I feel today?

_____

_____

_____

What am I grateful for today?

_____

_____

_____

What challenged me today?

_____

_____

_____

How can I overcome that challenge?

_____

_____

_____

What did I savor today?

_____

_____

_____

_____

BUILDING *the* BEST YOU THERE IS

What did I do today?

_____

_____

_____

What did I feel today?

_____

_____

_____

What am I grateful for today?

_____

_____

_____

What challenged me today?

_____

_____

_____

How can I overcome that challenge?

_____

_____

_____

What did I savor today?

_____

_____

_____

What did I do today?

_____

_____

_____

What did I feel today?

_____

_____

_____

What am I grateful for today?

_____

_____

_____

What challenged me today?

_____

_____

_____

How can I overcome that challenge?

_____

_____

_____

What did I savor today?

_____

_____

_____

YEAR ONE

YEAR TWO

BUILDING *the* BEST YOU THERE IS

What did I do today?

What did I do today?

What did I feel today?

What did I feel today?

What am I grateful for today?

What am I grateful for today?

What challenged me today?

What challenged me today?

How can I overcome that challenge?

How can I overcome that challenge?

What did I savor today?

What did I savor today?

YEAR ONE

YEAR TWO

BUILDING *the* BEST YOU THERE IS

What did I do today? _____

What did I do today? _____

What did I feel today? _____

What did I feel today? _____

What am I grateful for today? _____

What am I grateful for today? _____

What challenged me today? _____

What challenged me today? _____

How can I overcome that challenge? _____

How can I overcome that challenge? _____

What did I savor today? _____

What did I savor today? _____

What did I do today?

What did I do today?

What did I feel today?

What did I feel today?

What am I grateful for today?

What am I grateful for today?

What challenged me today?

What challenged me today?

How can I overcome that challenge?

How can I overcome that challenge?

What did I savor today?

What did I savor today?

BUILDING *the* BEST YOU THERE IS

What did I do today?

What did I do today?

What did I feel today?

What did I feel today?

What am I grateful for today?

What am I grateful for today?

What challenged me today?

What challenged me today?

How can I overcome that challenge?

How can I overcome that challenge?

What did I savor today?

What did I savor today?

BUILDING *the* BEST YOU THERE IS

Date

What did I do today?

What did I feel today?

What am I grateful for today?

What challenged me today?

How can I overcome that challenge?

What did I savor today?

YEAR ONE

Date

What did I do today?

What did I feel today?

What am I grateful for today?

What challenged me today?

How can I overcome that challenge?

What did I savor today?

YEAR TWO

BUILDING _the_ BEST YOU THERE IS

What did I do today?

What did I do today?

What did I feel today?

What did I feel today?

What am I grateful for today?

What am I grateful for today?

What challenged me today?

What challenged me today?

How can I overcome that challenge?

How can I overcome that challenge?

What did I savor today?

What did I savor today?

BUILDING *the* BEST YOU THERE IS

What did I do today?   *What did I do today?*

_____   _____

_____   _____

_____   _____

What did I feel today?   *What did I feel today?*

_____   _____

_____   _____

_____   _____

What am I grateful for today?   *What am I grateful for today?*

_____   _____

_____   _____

_____   _____

What challenged me today?   *What challenged me today?*

_____   _____

_____   _____

_____   _____

How can I overcome that challenge?   *How can I overcome that challenge?*

_____   _____

_____   _____

_____   _____

What did I savor today?   *What did I savor today?*

_____   _____

_____   _____

_____   _____

What did I do today?

What did I do today?

What did I feel today?

What did I feel today?

What am I grateful for today?

What am I grateful for today?

What challenged me today?

What challenged me today?

How can I overcome that challenge?

How can I overcome that challenge?

What did I savor today?

What did I savor today?

What did I do today?

_____

_____

_____

What did I feel today?

_____

_____

_____

What am I grateful for today?

_____

_____

_____

What challenged me today?

_____

_____

_____

How can I overcome that challenge?

_____

_____

_____

What did I savor today?

_____

_____

_____

What did I do today?

_____

_____

_____

What did I feel today?

_____

_____

_____

What am I grateful for today?

_____

_____

_____

What challenged me today?

_____

_____

_____

How can I overcome that challenge?

_____

_____

_____

What did I savor today?

_____

_____

_____

What did I do today?

_____

_____

_____

What did I feel today?

_____

_____

_____

What am I grateful for today?

_____

_____

_____

What challenged me today?

_____

_____

_____

How can I overcome that challenge?

_____

_____

_____

What did I savor today?

_____

_____

_____

_____

What did I do today?

_____

_____

_____

What did I feel today?

_____

_____

_____

What am I grateful for today?

_____

_____

_____

What challenged me today?

_____

_____

_____

How can I overcome that challenge?

_____

_____

_____

What did I savor today?

_____

_____

_____

_____

YEAR ONE   YEAR TWO

What did I do today?

_____

_____

_____

What did I feel today?

_____

_____

_____

What am I grateful for today?

_____

_____

_____

What challenged me today?

_____

_____

_____

How can I overcome that challenge?

_____

_____

_____

What did I savor today?

_____

_____

_____

What did I do today?

_____

_____

_____

What did I feel today?

_____

_____

_____

What am I grateful for today?

_____

_____

_____

What challenged me today?

_____

_____

_____

How can I overcome that challenge?

_____

_____

_____

What did I savor today?

_____

_____

_____

YEAR ONE

YEAR TWO

BUILDING *the* BEST YOU THERE IS

What did I do today?

_____

_____

_____

What did I feel today?

_____

_____

_____

What am I grateful for today?

_____

_____

_____

What challenged me today?

_____

_____

_____

How can I overcome that challenge?

_____

_____

_____

What did I savor today?

_____

_____

_____

What did I do today?

_____

_____

_____

What did I feel today?

_____

_____

_____

What am I grateful for today?

_____

_____

_____

What challenged me today?

_____

_____

_____

How can I overcome that challenge?

_____

_____

_____

What did I savor today?

_____

_____

_____

YEAR ONE

YEAR TWO

What did I do today?

What did I do today?

What did I feel today?

What did I feel today?

What am I grateful for today?

What am I grateful for today?

What challenged me today?

What challenged me today?

How can I overcome that challenge?

How can I overcome that challenge?

What did I savor today?

What did I savor today?

BUILDING _the_ BEST YOU THERE IS

What did I do today?

What did I feel today?

What am I grateful for today?

What challenged me today?

How can I overcome that challenge?

What did I savor today?

What did I do today?

What did I feel today?

What am I grateful for today?

What challenged me today?

How can I overcome that challenge?

What did I savor today?

BUILDING *the* BEST YOU THERE IS

What did I do today?

_____

_____

_____

What did I feel today?

_____

_____

_____

What am I grateful for today?

_____

_____

_____

What challenged me today?

_____

_____

_____

How can I overcome that challenge?

_____

_____

_____

What did I savor today?

_____

_____

_____

What did I do today?

_____

_____

_____

What did I feel today?

_____

_____

_____

What am I grateful for today?

_____

_____

_____

What challenged me today?

_____

_____

_____

How can I overcome that challenge?

_____

_____

_____

What did I savor today?

_____

_____

_____

YEAR ONE

YEAR TWO

BUILDING *the* BEST YOU THERE IS

What did I do today?

_____

_____

_____

What did I feel today?

_____

_____

_____

What am I grateful for today?

_____

_____

_____

What challenged me today?

_____

_____

_____

How can I overcome that challenge?

_____

_____

_____

What did I savor today?

_____

_____

_____

What did I do today?

_____

_____

_____

What did I feel today?

_____

_____

_____

What am I grateful for today?

_____

_____

_____

What challenged me today?

_____

_____

_____

How can I overcome that challenge?

_____

_____

_____

What did I savor today?

_____

_____

_____

YEAR ONE

YEAR TWO

BUILDING *the* BEST YOU THERE IS

What did I do today?

_____

_____

_____

What did I feel today?

_____

_____

_____

What am I grateful for today?

_____

_____

_____

What challenged me today?

_____

_____

_____

How can I overcome that challenge?

_____

_____

_____

What did I savor today?

_____

_____

_____

What did I do today?

_____

_____

_____

What did I feel today?

_____

_____

_____

What am I grateful for today?

_____

_____

_____

What challenged me today?

_____

_____

_____

How can I overcome that challenge?

_____

_____

_____

What did I savor today?

_____

_____

_____

YEAR ONE

YEAR TWO

What did I do today?

_____

_____

_____

What did I feel today?

_____

_____

_____

What am I grateful for today?

_____

_____

_____

What challenged me today?

_____

_____

_____

How can I overcome that challenge?

_____

_____

_____

What did I savor today?

_____

_____

_____

_____

What did I do today?

_____

_____

_____

What did I feel today?

_____

_____

_____

What am I grateful for today?

_____

_____

_____

What challenged me today?

_____

_____

_____

How can I overcome that challenge?

_____

_____

_____

What did I savor today?

_____

_____

_____

_____

Date

What did I do today?

What did I feel today?

What am I grateful for today?

What challenged me today?

How can I overcome that challenge?

What did I savor today?

Date

What did I do today?

What did I feel today?

What am I grateful for today?

What challenged me today?

How can I overcome that challenge?

What did I savor today?

What did I do today?

What did I do today?

What did I feel today?

What did I feel today?

What am I grateful for today?

What am I grateful for today?

What challenged me today?

What challenged me today?

How can I overcome that challenge?

How can I overcome that challenge?

What did I savor today?

What did I savor today?

BUILDING *the* BEST YOU THERE IS

What did I do today?

What did I feel today?

What am I grateful for today?

What challenged me today?

How can I overcome that challenge?

What did I savor today?

What did I do today?

What did I feel today?

What am I grateful for today?

What challenged me today?

How can I overcome that challenge?

What did I savor today?

BUILDING *the* BEST YOU THERE IS

What did I do today?

What did I do today?

What did I feel today?

What did I feel today?

What am I grateful for today?

What am I grateful for today?

What challenged me today?

What challenged me today?

How can I overcome that challenge?

How can I overcome that challenge?

What did I savor today?

What did I savor today?

_____ Date

What did I do today?
_____
_____
_____
_____

What did I feel today?
_____
_____
_____

What am I grateful for today?
_____
_____
_____

What challenged me today?
_____
_____
_____

How can I overcome that challenge?
_____
_____
_____

What did I savor today?
_____
_____
_____

_____ Date

What did I do today?
_____
_____
_____
_____

What did I feel today?
_____
_____
_____

What am I grateful for today?
_____
_____
_____

What challenged me today?
_____
_____
_____

How can I overcome that challenge?
_____
_____
_____

What did I savor today?
_____
_____
_____

What did I do today?   What did I do today?

_____   _____

_____   _____

_____   _____

What did I feel today?   What did I feel today?

_____   _____

_____   _____

_____   _____

What am I grateful for today?   What am I grateful for today?

_____   _____

_____   _____

_____   _____

What challenged me today?   What challenged me today?

_____   _____

_____   _____

_____   _____

How can I overcome that challenge?   How can I overcome that challenge?

_____   _____

_____   _____

_____   _____

What did I savor today?   What did I savor today?

_____   _____

_____   _____

_____   _____

YEAR ONE   YEAR TWO

BUILDING *the* BEST YOU THERE IS

Date

Date

What did I do today?

What did I do today?

What did I feel today?

What did I feel today?

What am I grateful for today?

What am I grateful for today?

What challenged me today?

What challenged me today?

How can I overcome that challenge?

How can I overcome that challenge?

What did I savor today?

What did I savor today?

BUILDING *the* BEST YOU THERE IS

What did I do today?

What did I do today?

What did I feel today?

What did I feel today?

What am I grateful for today?

What am I grateful for today?

What challenged me today?

What challenged me today?

How can I overcome that challenge?

How can I overcome that challenge?

What did I savor today?

What did I savor today?

What did I do today?

What did I do today?

What did I feel today?

What did I feel today?

What am I grateful for today?

What am I grateful for today?

What challenged me today?

What challenged me today?

How can I overcome that challenge?

How can I overcome that challenge?

What did I savor today?

What did I savor today?

What did I do today?

What did I feel today?

What am I grateful for today?

What challenged me today?

How can I overcome that challenge?

What did I savor today?

What did I do today?

What did I feel today?

What am I grateful for today?

What challenged me today?

How can I overcome that challenge?

What did I savor today?

What did I do today?

_____

_____

_____

What did I feel today?

_____

_____

_____

What am I grateful for today?

_____

_____

_____

What challenged me today?

_____

_____

_____

How can I overcome that challenge?

_____

_____

_____

What did I savor today?

_____

_____

_____

What did I do today?

_____

_____

_____

What did I feel today?

_____

_____

_____

What am I grateful for today?

_____

_____

_____

What challenged me today?

_____

_____

_____

How can I overcome that challenge?

_____

_____

_____

What did I savor today?

_____

_____

_____

BUILDING *the* BEST YOU THERE IS

What did I do today?

What did I do today?

What did I feel today?

What did I feel today?

What am I grateful for today?

What am I grateful for today?

What challenged me today?

What challenged me today?

How can I overcome that challenge?

How can I overcome that challenge?

What did I savor today?

What did I savor today?

BUILDING *the* BEST YOU THERE IS

What did I do today?

What did I do today?

What did I feel today?

What did I feel today?

What am I grateful for today?

What am I grateful for today?

What challenged me today?

What challenged me today?

How can I overcome that challenge?

How can I overcome that challenge?

What did I savor today?

What did I savor today?

BUILDING *the* BEST YOU THERE IS

What did I do today?

What did I do today?

_____

_____

_____

_____

What did I feel today?

What did I feel today?

_____

_____

_____

_____

What am I grateful for today?

What am I grateful for today?

_____

_____

_____

_____

What challenged me today?

What challenged me today?

_____

_____

_____

_____

How can I overcome that challenge?

How can I overcome that challenge?

_____

_____

_____

_____

What did I savor today?

What did I savor today?

_____

_____

_____

_____

_____

_____

What did I do today?

_____

_____

_____

What did I feel today?

_____

_____

What am I grateful for today?

_____

_____

_____

What challenged me today?

_____

_____

How can I overcome that challenge?

_____

_____

_____

What did I savor today?

_____

_____

_____

What did I do today?

_____

_____

_____

What did I feel today?

_____

_____

What am I grateful for today?

_____

_____

_____

What challenged me today?

_____

_____

How can I overcome that challenge?

_____

_____

_____

What did I savor today?

_____

_____

_____

YEAR ONE

YEAR TWO

BUILDING *the* BEST YOU THERE IS

What do I value most in life?

_____
_____
_____
_____
_____

Am I influenced by material things?

_____
_____
_____
_____
_____

Do I treasure family?

_____
_____
_____
_____
_____

What do I admire most about others?

_____
_____
_____
_____
_____

How do I picture myself in twenty years?

_____
_____
_____
_____
_____

How do I get there?

_____
_____
_____
_____
_____

Am I bound to the past?

_____
_____
_____
_____

Do I repeat old patterns?

_____
_____
_____
_____

Do I long for a new direction?

_____
_____
_____
_____

What is that direction?

_____
_____
_____
_____

How do I get there?

_____
_____
_____
_____

What's my first step to take?

_____
_____
_____
_____

What do I value most in life?

_____

_____

_____

_____

Am I influenced by material things?

_____

_____

_____

_____

Do I treasure family?

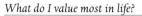

_____

_____

_____

_____

What do I admire most about others?

_____

_____

_____

_____

How do I picture myself in twenty years?

_____

_____

_____

_____

How do I get there?

_____

_____

_____

_____

_____

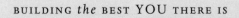

Am I bound to the past?

_____

_____

_____

_____

Do I repeat old patterns?

_____

_____

_____

_____

Do I long for a new direction?

_____

_____

_____

_____

What is that direction?

_____

_____

_____

_____

How do I get there?

_____

_____

_____

_____

What's my first step to take?

_____

_____

_____

_____

Date _____

What did I do today? _____

_____

_____

_____

What did I feel today? _____

_____

_____

_____

What am I grateful for today? _____

_____

_____

_____

_____

What challenged me today? _____

_____

_____

_____

How can I overcome that challenge? _____

_____

_____

_____

What did I savor today? _____

_____

_____

_____

_____

Date _____

What did I do today? _____

_____

_____

_____

What did I feel today? _____

_____

_____

_____

What am I grateful for today? _____

_____

_____

_____

_____

What challenged me today? _____

_____

_____

_____

How can I overcome that challenge? _____

_____

_____

_____

What did I savor today? _____

_____

_____

_____

_____

YEAR ONE

YEAR TWO

BUILDING *the* BEST YOU THERE IS

What did I do today?   *What did I do today?*

_____   _____

_____   _____

_____   _____

What did I feel today?   *What did I feel today?*

_____   _____

_____   _____

_____   _____

What am I grateful for today?   *What am I grateful for today?*

_____   _____

_____   _____

_____   _____

What challenged me today?   *What challenged me today?*

_____   _____

_____   _____

_____   _____

How can I overcome that challenge?   *How can I overcome that challenge?*

_____   _____

_____   _____

_____   _____

What did I savor today?   *What did I savor today?*

_____   _____

_____   _____

_____   _____

YEAR ONE   YEAR TWO

BUILDING *the* BEST YOU THERE IS

What did I do today?

_____

_____

_____

What did I feel today?

_____

_____

_____

What am I grateful for today?

_____

_____

_____

What challenged me today?

_____

_____

_____

How can I overcome that challenge?

_____

_____

_____

What did I savor today?

_____

_____

_____

_____

What did I do today?

_____

_____

_____

What did I feel today?

_____

_____

_____

What am I grateful for today?

_____

_____

_____

What challenged me today?

_____

_____

_____

How can I overcome that challenge?

_____

_____

_____

What did I savor today?

_____

_____

_____

_____

YEAR ONE

YEAR TWO

BUILDING *the* BEST YOU THERE IS

What did I do today?

_____

_____

_____

What did I feel today?

_____

_____

_____

What am I grateful for today?

_____

_____

_____

What challenged me today?

_____

_____

_____

How can I overcome that challenge?

_____

_____

_____

What did I savor today?

_____

_____

_____

What did I do today?

_____

_____

_____

What did I feel today?

_____

_____

_____

What am I grateful for today?

_____

_____

_____

What challenged me today?

_____

_____

_____

How can I overcome that challenge?

_____

_____

_____

What did I savor today?

_____

_____

_____

What did I do today?

_____

_____

_____

What did I feel today?

_____

_____

_____

What am I grateful for today?

_____

_____

_____

What challenged me today?

_____

_____

_____

How can I overcome that challenge?

_____

_____

_____

What did I savor today?

_____

_____

_____

_____

What did I do today?

_____

_____

_____

What did I feel today?

_____

_____

_____

What am I grateful for today?

_____

_____

_____

What challenged me today?

_____

_____

_____

How can I overcome that challenge?

_____

_____

_____

What did I savor today?

_____

_____

_____

_____

BUILDING *the* BEST YOU THERE IS

What did I do today?

_____

_____

_____

What did I feel today?

_____

_____

_____

What am I grateful for today?

_____

_____

_____

What challenged me today?

_____

_____

_____

How can I overcome that challenge?

_____

_____

_____

What did I savor today?

_____

_____

_____

What did I do today?

_____

_____

_____

What did I feel today?

_____

_____

_____

What am I grateful for today?

_____

_____

_____

What challenged me today?

_____

_____

_____

How can I overcome that challenge?

_____

_____

_____

What did I savor today?

_____

_____

_____

YEAR ONE

YEAR TWO

BUILDING _the_ BEST YOU THERE IS

What did I do today?

_____

_____

_____

What did I feel today?

_____

_____

_____

What am I grateful for today?

_____

_____

_____

What challenged me today?

_____

_____

_____

How can I overcome that challenge?

_____

_____

_____

What did I savor today?

_____

_____

_____

What did I do today?

_____

_____

_____

What did I feel today?

_____

_____

_____

What am I grateful for today?

_____

_____

_____

What challenged me today?

_____

_____

_____

How can I overcome that challenge?

_____

_____

_____

What did I savor today?

_____

_____

_____

YEAR ONE

YEAR TWO

What did I do today?

_____

_____

_____

What did I feel today?

_____

_____

_____

What am I grateful for today?

_____

_____

_____

What challenged me today?

_____

_____

_____

How can I overcome that challenge?

_____

_____

_____

What did I savor today?

_____

_____

_____

What did I do today?

_____

_____

_____

What did I feel today?

_____

_____

_____

What am I grateful for today?

_____

_____

_____

What challenged me today?

_____

_____

_____

How can I overcome that challenge?

_____

_____

_____

What did I savor today?

_____

_____

_____

BUILDING *the* BEST YOU THERE IS

What did I do today?

What did I feel today?

What am I grateful for today?

What challenged me today?

How can I overcome that challenge?

What did I savor today?

BUILDING *the* BEST YOU THERE IS

What did I do today?

What did I feel today?

What am I grateful for today?

What challenged me today?

How can I overcome that challenge?

What did I savor today?

What did I do today?

What did I feel today?

What am I grateful for today?

What challenged me today?

How can I overcome that challenge?

What did I savor today?

What did I do today?

What did I feel today?

What am I grateful for today?

What challenged me today?

How can I overcome that challenge?

What did I savor today?

What did I do today?

What did I feel today?

What am I grateful for today?

What challenged me today?

How can I overcome that challenge?

What did I savor today?

BUILDING *the* BEST YOU THERE IS

What did I do today?

_____

_____

_____

What did I feel today?

_____

_____

_____

What am I grateful for today?

_____

_____

_____

What challenged me today?

_____

_____

_____

How can I overcome that challenge?

_____

_____

_____

What did I savor today?

_____

_____

_____

What did I do today?

_____

_____

_____

What did I feel today?

_____

_____

_____

What am I grateful for today?

_____

_____

_____

What challenged me today?

_____

_____

_____

How can I overcome that challenge?

_____

_____

_____

What did I savor today?

_____

_____

_____

BUILDING *the* BEST YOU THERE IS

What did I do today?

_____

_____

_____

What did I feel today?

_____

_____

_____

What am I grateful for today?

_____

_____

_____

What challenged me today?

_____

_____

_____

How can I overcome that challenge?

_____

_____

_____

What did I savor today?

_____

_____

_____

_____

What did I do today?

_____

_____

_____

What did I feel today?

_____

_____

_____

What am I grateful for today?

_____

_____

_____

What challenged me today?

_____

_____

_____

How can I overcome that challenge?

_____

_____

_____

What did I savor today?

_____

_____

_____

_____

YEAR ONE   YEAR TWO

What did I do today?

What did I do today?

_____

_____

_____

_____

What did I feel today?

What did I feel today?

_____

_____

_____

_____

What am I grateful for today?

What am I grateful for today?

_____

_____

_____

_____

What challenged me today?

What challenged me today?

_____

_____

_____

_____

How can I overcome that challenge?

How can I overcome that challenge?

_____

_____

_____

_____

What did I savor today?

What did I savor today?

_____

_____

_____

_____

What did I do today?

What did I feel today?

What am I grateful for today?

What challenged me today?

How can I overcome that challenge?

What did I savor today?

What did I do today?

What did I feel today?

What am I grateful for today?

What challenged me today?

How can I overcome that challenge?

What did I savor today?

What did I do today?

What did I do today?

_____

_____

_____

_____

What did I feel today?

What did I feel today?

_____

_____

_____

_____

What am I grateful for today?

What am I grateful for today?

_____

_____

_____

_____

What challenged me today?

What challenged me today?

_____

_____

_____

_____

How can I overcome that challenge?

How can I overcome that challenge?

_____

_____

_____

_____

What did I savor today?

What did I savor today?

_____

_____

_____

_____

What did I do today?

_____

_____

_____

What did I feel today?

_____

_____

_____

What am I grateful for today?

_____

_____

_____

What challenged me today?

_____

_____

_____

How can I overcome that challenge?

_____

_____

_____

What did I savor today?

_____

_____

_____

_____

What did I do today?

_____

_____

_____

What did I feel today?

_____

_____

_____

What am I grateful for today?

_____

_____

_____

What challenged me today?

_____

_____

_____

How can I overcome that challenge?

_____

_____

_____

What did I savor today?

_____

_____

_____

_____

What did I do today?

_____

_____

_____

What did I feel today?

_____

_____

_____

What am I grateful for today?

_____

_____

_____

What challenged me today?

_____

_____

_____

How can I overcome that challenge?

_____

_____

_____

What did I savor today?

_____

_____

_____

What did I do today?

_____

_____

_____

What did I feel today?

_____

_____

_____

What am I grateful for today?

_____

_____

_____

What challenged me today?

_____

_____

_____

How can I overcome that challenge?

_____

_____

_____

What did I savor today?

_____

_____

_____

YEAR ONE

YEAR TWO

What did I do today?

_____

_____

_____

What did I feel today?

_____

_____

_____

What am I grateful for today?

_____

_____

_____

What challenged me today?

_____

_____

_____

How can I overcome that challenge?

_____

_____

_____

What did I savor today?

_____

_____

_____

What did I do today?

_____

_____

_____

What did I feel today?

_____

_____

_____

What am I grateful for today?

_____

_____

_____

What challenged me today?

_____

_____

_____

How can I overcome that challenge?

_____

_____

_____

What did I savor today?

_____

_____

_____

YEAR ONE

YEAR TWO

BUILDING *the* BEST YOU THERE IS

What did I do today?

_____

_____

_____

_____

What did I feel today?

_____

_____

_____

_____

What am I grateful for today?

_____

_____

_____

_____

What challenged me today?

_____

_____

_____

_____

How can I overcome that challenge?

_____

_____

_____

_____

What did I savor today?

_____

_____

_____

_____

YEAR ONE

What did I do today?

_____

_____

_____

_____

What did I feel today?

_____

_____

_____

_____

What am I grateful for today?

_____

_____

_____

_____

What challenged me today?

_____

_____

_____

_____

How can I overcome that challenge?

_____

_____

_____

_____

What did I savor today?

_____

_____

_____

_____

YEAR TWO

BUILDING *the* BEST YOU THERE IS

What did I do today?

_____

_____

_____

What did I feel today?

_____

_____

_____

What am I grateful for today?

_____

_____

_____

What challenged me today?

_____

_____

_____

How can I overcome that challenge?

_____

_____

_____

What did I savor today?

_____

_____

_____

What did I do today?

_____

_____

_____

What did I feel today?

_____

_____

_____

What am I grateful for today?

_____

_____

_____

What challenged me today?

_____

_____

_____

How can I overcome that challenge?

_____

_____

_____

What did I savor today?

_____

_____

_____

YEAR ONE   YEAR TWO

What did I do today?

What did I do today?

What did I feel today?

What did I feel today?

What am I grateful for today?

What am I grateful for today?

What challenged me today?

What challenged me today?

How can I overcome that challenge?

How can I overcome that challenge?

What did I savor today?

What did I savor today?

What did I do today?

What did I do today?

_____

_____

_____

_____

_____

_____

What did I feel today?

What did I feel today?

_____

_____

_____

_____

_____

_____

What am I grateful for today?

What am I grateful for today?

_____

_____

_____

_____

_____

_____

What challenged me today?

What challenged me today?

_____

_____

_____

_____

_____

_____

How can I overcome that challenge?

How can I overcome that challenge?

_____

_____

_____

_____

_____

_____

What did I savor today?

What did I savor today?

_____

_____

_____

_____

_____

_____

Year One

Year Two

BUILDING *the* BEST YOU THERE IS

What did I do today?

What did I do today?

What did I feel today?

What did I feel today?

What am I grateful for today?

What am I grateful for today?

What challenged me today?

What challenged me today?

How can I overcome that challenge?

How can I overcome that challenge?

What did I savor today?

What did I savor today?

What did I do today?

_____

_____

_____

_____

What did I feel today?

_____

_____

_____

What am I grateful for today?

_____

_____

_____

What challenged me today?

_____

_____

_____

How can I overcome that challenge?

_____

_____

_____

What did I savor today?

_____

_____

_____

What did I do today?

_____

_____

_____

_____

What did I feel today?

_____

_____

_____

What am I grateful for today?

_____

_____

_____

What challenged me today?

_____

_____

_____

How can I overcome that challenge?

_____

_____

_____

What did I savor today?

_____

_____

_____

YEAR ONE

YEAR TWO

BUILDING *the* BEST YOU THERE IS

What did I do today?

_____

_____

_____

What did I feel today?

_____

_____

_____

What am I grateful for today?

_____

_____

_____

What challenged me today?

_____

_____

_____

How can I overcome that challenge?

_____

_____

_____

What did I savor today?

_____

_____

_____

What did I do today?

_____

_____

_____

What did I feel today?

_____

_____

_____

What am I grateful for today?

_____

_____

_____

What challenged me today?

_____

_____

_____

How can I overcome that challenge?

_____

_____

_____

What did I savor today?

_____

_____

_____

What did I do today?

What did I do today?

What did I feel today?

What did I feel today?

What am I grateful for today?

What am I grateful for today?

What challenged me today?

What challenged me today?

How can I overcome that challenge?

How can I overcome that challenge?

What did I savor today?

What did I savor today?

BUILDING *the* BEST YOU THERE IS

_____
Date

What did I do today?

_____

_____

_____

_____

What did I feel today?

_____

_____

_____

_____

What am I grateful for today?

_____

_____

_____

_____

What challenged me today?

_____

_____

_____

_____

How can I overcome that challenge?

_____

_____

_____

_____

What did I savor today?

_____

_____

_____

_____

_____
Date

What did I do today?

_____

_____

_____

_____

What did I feel today?

_____

_____

_____

_____

What am I grateful for today?

_____

_____

_____

_____

What challenged me today?

_____

_____

_____

_____

How can I overcome that challenge?

_____

_____

_____

_____

What did I savor today?

_____

_____

_____

_____

_____ Date

_____ Date

What did I do today?
_____
_____
_____
_____

What did I feel today?
_____
_____
_____
_____

What am I grateful for today?
_____
_____
_____
_____

What challenged me today?
_____
_____
_____
_____

How can I overcome that challenge?
_____
_____
_____
_____

What did I savor today?
_____
_____
_____
_____
_____

YEAR ONE

What did I do today?
_____
_____
_____
_____

What did I feel today?
_____
_____
_____
_____

What am I grateful for today?
_____
_____
_____
_____

What challenged me today?
_____
_____
_____
_____

How can I overcome that challenge?
_____
_____
_____
_____

What did I savor today?
_____
_____
_____
_____
_____

YEAR TWO

BUILDING *the* BEST YOU THERE IS

Date

What did I do today?

What did I feel today?

What am I grateful for today?

What challenged me today?

How can I overcome that challenge?

What did I savor today?

Date

What did I do today?

What did I feel today?

What am I grateful for today?

What challenged me today?

How can I overcome that challenge?

What did I savor today?

What did I do today?	*What did I do today?*
_____	_____
_____	_____
_____	_____
_____	_____
What did I feel today?	*What did I feel today?*
_____	_____
_____	_____
_____	_____
_____	_____
What am I grateful for today?	*What am I grateful for today?*
_____	_____
_____	_____
_____	_____
_____	_____
What challenged me today?	*What challenged me today?*
_____	_____
_____	_____
_____	_____
_____	_____
How can I overcome that challenge?	*How can I overcome that challenge?*
_____	_____
_____	_____
_____	_____
_____	_____
What did I savor today?	*What did I savor today?*
_____	_____
_____	_____
_____	_____
_____	_____

What did I do today?

What did I feel today?

What am I grateful for today?

What challenged me today?

How can I overcome that challenge?

What did I savor today?

What did I do today?

What did I feel today?

What am I grateful for today?

What challenged me today?

How can I overcome that challenge?

What did I savor today?

What did I do today?

What did I feel today?

What am I grateful for today?

What challenged me today?

How can I overcome that challenge?

What did I savor today?

What did I do today?

What did I feel today?

What am I grateful for today?

What challenged me today?

How can I overcome that challenge?

What did I savor today?

BUILDING *the* BEST YOU THERE IS

What did I do today?

_____

_____

_____

_____

What did I feel today?

_____

_____

_____

_____

What am I grateful for today?

_____

_____

_____

_____

What challenged me today?

_____

_____

_____

_____

How can I overcome that challenge?

_____

_____

_____

_____

What did I savor today?

_____

_____

_____

_____

YEAR ONE

What did I do today?

_____

_____

_____

_____

What did I feel today?

_____

_____

_____

_____

What am I grateful for today?

_____

_____

_____

_____

What challenged me today?

_____

_____

_____

_____

How can I overcome that challenge?

_____

_____

_____

_____

What did I savor today?

_____

_____

_____

_____

YEAR TWO

What did I do today?

What did I feel today?

What am I grateful for today?

What challenged me today?

How can I overcome that challenge?

What did I savor today?

What did I do today?

What did I feel today?

What am I grateful for today?

What challenged me today?

How can I overcome that challenge?

What did I savor today?

What did I do today?

_____

_____

_____

_____

What did I feel today?

_____

_____

_____

_____

What am I grateful for today?

_____

_____

_____

_____

What challenged me today?

_____

_____

_____

_____

How can I overcome that challenge?

_____

_____

_____

_____

What did I savor today?

_____

_____

_____

_____

What did I do today?

_____

_____

_____

_____

What did I feel today?

_____

_____

_____

_____

What am I grateful for today?

_____

_____

_____

_____

What challenged me today?

_____

_____

_____

_____

How can I overcome that challenge?

_____

_____

_____

_____

What did I savor today?

_____

_____

_____

_____

What did I do today?

_____

_____

_____

What did I feel today?

_____

_____

_____

What am I grateful for today?

_____

_____

_____

What challenged me today?

_____

_____

_____

How can I overcome that challenge?

_____

_____

_____

What did I savor today?

_____

_____

_____

YEAR ONE

Date

What did I do today?

_____

_____

_____

What did I feel today?

_____

_____

_____

What am I grateful for today?

_____

_____

_____

What challenged me today?

_____

_____

_____

How can I overcome that challenge?

_____

_____

_____

What did I savor today?

_____

_____

_____

YEAR TWO

What did I do today?

_____

_____

_____

What did I feel today?

_____

_____

_____

What am I grateful for today?

_____

_____

_____

What challenged me today?

_____

_____

_____

How can I overcome that challenge?

_____

_____

_____

What did I savor today?

_____

_____

_____

What did I do today?

_____

_____

_____

What did I feel today?

_____

_____

_____

What am I grateful for today?

_____

_____

_____

What challenged me today?

_____

_____

_____

How can I overcome that challenge?

_____

_____

_____

What did I savor today?

_____

_____

_____

YEAR ONE

YEAR TWO

BUILDING *the* BEST YOU THERE IS

Date _____

What did I do today? _____
_____
_____
_____

What did I feel today? _____
_____
_____
_____

What am I grateful for today? _____
_____
_____
_____

What challenged me today? _____
_____
_____
_____

How can I overcome that challenge? _____
_____
_____
_____

What did I savor today? _____
_____
_____
_____

YEAR ONE

Date _____

What did I do today? _____
_____
_____
_____

What did I feel today? _____
_____
_____
_____

What am I grateful for today? _____
_____
_____
_____

What challenged me today? _____
_____
_____
_____

How can I overcome that challenge? _____
_____
_____
_____

What did I savor today? _____
_____
_____
_____

YEAR TWO

BUILDING *the* BEST YOU THERE IS

Date

What did I do today?

_____

_____

_____

_____

What did I feel today?

_____

_____

_____

What am I grateful for today?

_____

_____

_____

What challenged me today?

_____

_____

_____

How can I overcome that challenge?

_____

_____

_____

What did I savor today?

_____

_____

_____

YEAR ONE

Date

What did I do today?

_____

_____

_____

_____

What did I feel today?

_____

_____

_____

What am I grateful for today?

_____

_____

_____

What challenged me today?

_____

_____

_____

How can I overcome that challenge?

_____

_____

_____

What did I savor today?

_____

_____

_____

YEAR TWO

BUILDING _the_ BEST YOU THERE IS

What did I do today?

_____

_____

_____

What did I feel today?

_____

_____

_____

What am I grateful for today?

_____

_____

_____

What challenged me today?

_____

_____

_____

How can I overcome that challenge?

_____

_____

_____

What did I savor today?

_____

_____

_____

_____

YEAR ONE

What did I do today?

_____

_____

_____

What did I feel today?

_____

_____

_____

What am I grateful for today?

_____

_____

_____

What challenged me today?

_____

_____

_____

How can I overcome that challenge?

_____

_____

_____

What did I savor today?

_____

_____

_____

_____

YEAR TWO

BUILDING *the* BEST YOU THERE IS

Date
Date

What did I do today?

What did I do today?

What did I feel today?

What did I feel today?

What am I grateful for today?

What am I grateful for today?

What challenged me today?

What challenged me today?

How can I overcome that challenge?

How can I overcome that challenge?

What did I savor today?

What did I savor today?

YEAR ONE

YEAR TWO

BUILDING *the* BEST YOU THERE IS

What do I think of myself?

_____

_____

_____

_____

What do other people think of me?

_____

_____

_____

_____

Do I present my true self to others?

_____

_____

_____

_____

Do I show others that I care?

_____

_____

_____

_____

Do I listen to others?

_____

_____

_____

_____

How can I be more tuned in?

_____

_____

_____

_____

_____

BUILDING *the* BEST YOU THERE IS

Do I enjoy getting up in the morning?

_____

_____

_____

_____

Do I relish what I do?

_____

_____

_____

_____

Do I look forward to life?

_____

_____

_____

_____

What would resonate more with me?

_____

_____

_____

_____

Do I see the road to fulfillment?

_____

_____

_____

_____

How do I take that path?

_____

_____

_____

_____

What do I think of myself?

_____

_____

_____

_____

_____

What do other people think of me?

_____

_____

_____

_____

_____

Do I present my true self to others?

_____

_____

_____

_____

_____

Do I show others that I care?

_____

_____

_____

_____

_____

Do I listen to others?

_____

_____

_____

_____

_____

How can I be more tuned in?

_____

_____

_____

_____

_____

Do I enjoy getting up in the morning?

_____

_____

_____

_____

Do I relish what I do?

_____

_____

_____

_____

Do I look forward to life?

_____

_____

_____

_____

What would resonate more with me?

_____

_____

_____

_____

Do I see the road to fulfillment?

_____

_____

_____

_____

How do I take that path?

_____

_____

_____

_____